TREVOR A JARRETT

NEVER FORGET
What It's Like To Be A 'C'

WHY TEAMS AND ORGANISATIONS FAIL
THE SINGLE MOST IMPORTANT FACT TODAY'S
LEADERS NEED TO KNOW FOR THEIR TEAM
AND ORGANISATION TO PROSPER

THE FORGOTTEN FACTOR

authorHOUSE

AuthorHouse™ UK
1663 Liberty Drive
Bloomington, IN 47403 USA
www.authorhouse.co.uk
Phone: 0800.197.4150

© 2018 Trevor A Jarrett. All rights reserved.

Second Edition
First paperback printed in Great Britain in 2015 published by Stop Press Publications.

No part of this book may be reproduced, stored in a retrieval system, or transmitted by any means without the written permission of the author.

Published by AuthorHouse 01/22/2018

ISBN: 978-1-5462-8756-8 (sc)
ISBN: 978-1-5462-8757-5 (hc)
ISBN: 978-1-5462-8755-1 (e)

Print information available on the last page.

Any people depicted in stock imagery provided by Thinkstock are models, and such images are being used for illustrative purposes only.
Certain stock imagery © Thinkstock.

This book is printed on acid-free paper.

Because of the dynamic nature of the Internet, any web addresses or links contained in this book may have changed since publication and may no longer be valid. The views expressed in this work are solely those of the author and do not necessarily reflect the views of the publisher, and the publisher hereby disclaims any responsibility for them.

ACKNOWLEDGEMENTS

With thanks to everyone who has been a part of making this book happen, including Brian and his exec team who played the 'Game' with honesty, naivety and unbound enthusiasm.

A special thanks to Shaun Price who has worked with me over the last 12 years and has been an integral part of shaping the game into what it is today.

Even with Shaun Price, Brian Jeffers, his exec team, and every other team around the world that have experienced the 'Game', the first and last words would never have been penned without a kick up the backside from Chris, – you know who you are.

Where would I be without the support and help from Eagle Printers who have put up with constant changes and amendments to the original script and artwork.

A huge thanks go to May Corfield, my editor and Angela Baynham, my proofreader who both played an amazing part in taking something from a raw state of gibberish and making into something totally professional and readable – Thank you.

And finally, a huge thanks to Jane, my wife, who has put up with nearly nine months of listening to the tapping of a keyboard through rewrite after rewrite.

ABOUT THE AUTHOR

Banker, toilet-roll salesman, alcohol and cigarette sales management – these are just a few roles in Trevor Jarrett's background before he moved into the world of learning and development. There he discovered an adept ability to make a difference in people and in organisational lives.

Based in Billericay, Essex, UK, with his family, he is the Managing Director of Change Creation Limited, a leading learning and development organisation striving continually to seek new ways to inspire people to implement positive behavioural change within themselves and their organisations.

Described by his clients as a genuinely exceptional all-rounder, Trevor is an engaging facilitator, a results-focused coach and a motivational speaker.

He is driven by his positioning statement of indomitable yearning to make life-changing differences.

CONTENTS

Foreword xi
Introduction xiii

Before we Begin 1
A Chance Meeting 4
A Meeting not by Chance 11
Setting up the 'Game' 24
    The 'Game' 25
    The A 26
    The B 27
    The C 27
    The Set-up 28
    The Seating 28
Playing the 'Game' 34
Level feelings 44
    C-Level feelings 44
    B-Level feelings 48
    A-Level feelings 50
Summary 52
The Beginning of the End 56
Retrospection is a Wonderful Thing 71
    What A could have done differently 71
    What the Bs could have done differently 79
    What the Cs could have done differently 84
Capturing the Moment 91
Closing Speech 95

FOREWORD

When taking advice on how I should structure the foreword of this book, it was suggested I 'show the reader why Trevor has the proper credibility to have written this book'. This gave me some comfort, as the book is based on many years of playing 'the Game' during the numerous leadership workshops that Trevor and I have delivered to blue chip companies over the past 12 years.

We originally saw an abridged version on a visit to the US many years ago and began using it as an ice breaker or energiser. However, it soon became clear that the impact on the participants and the resulting learning points were more powerful than we had initially imagined. It was then that we developed the activity into a full-scale business simulation game, which became the keystone of our leadership workshops. I recall being present when the phrase 'Never Forget What It's Like To Be A C' was first voiced and it is without doubt the perfect title for this book, as it sums up the key message from the story you are about to read. It may not mean much to you now, but remember that the title of the book Who Moved My Cheese? meant little to any of us, until we had read the whole story!

Whether you are a management trainee, team leader, middle manager, senior manager, managing director or CEO, this story has a message for you that will strike right to the core of your team, whatever the size.

Finally, it is only appropriate that we thank the participants who have taken part in the enormous amount of fun and synergy we have had in evolving this activity far beyond our original expectations. At the last count, this number runs at approximately

2,000 people and I am sure they will all recall that every time we facilitated the Game, the feedback we received was either "this is our company!" or "this is my team!". This confirmed that the Game was clearly delivering a reflection of reality. As the narrative unfolds, I implore you to reflect on the way you communicate within your own business, and ask yourself if you've actually forgotten what it's like to be a 'C'?

Shaun Price
Director of Change Creation

INTRODUCTION

According to recent research*, nearly 40 per cent of new chief executives fail completely within the first 18 months of their tenure. It's a frightening statistic and could be a key indicator as to why many organisations fail.

If we live by the adage that we all learn from failure and move forward, are our chief executives moving forward? Have they learnt from their failures? I believe an effective leader must learn from the mistakes he or she makes, but often people seem to make the same mistakes time and time again. Moreover, there are leadership failures that can easily weaken an organisation and ultimately paralyse its ability to perform. With any failure in leadership, it is important to understand what's behind it. These failures are often the root causes that prevent leaders and their organisations from moving forward, and the subsequent barriers restrict an organisation's ability to creatively seek new opportunities.

It's not just about the leader, though. Everyone in the organisation can feel the impact of failure. Often failure will be attributed to the leader and, in particular, those who are either lacking the appropriate leadership attributes or who fail to abide by the right leadership principles. Either way, they are setting themselves up to fail by slipping back into their old habits.

Primarily, leaders need to understand that their leadership skills will be constantly challenged in an ever-changing, complex work environment and they can very quickly, and subconsciously, develop an organisational situation that demonstrates a real leadership failure and leaves their employees with a feeling of desolation.

Paradoxically, it is recognised that most people want to do their best in the workplace – it's time that leaders appreciated this and applied some basic principles to the way they engage their people.

---

* Why Do 40% of Executives Fail? By Stephen Harvard Davis

BEFORE WE BEGIN

On reflection, it wasn't all that difficult to decide what to call this book. You see, I always wanted to write a book that makes some sense of why many teams, and ultimately organisations, fail. My experience suggests there is one single but vital factor that many leaders tend to forget as they pursue successful careers.

Consequently, the title needed to describe the single most important factor all leaders, and ultimately their organisations, need to know to get themselves, their teams and their organisations back on track before it's too late.

Never Forget What It's Like To Be A 'C' identifies 'The Forgotten Factor' and takes you on a journey that will help identify where leaders are perhaps failing their people.

The title is designed to be provocative whilst memorable, the content to be thought-provoking but understandable, and the message to be reality based on experience.

Okay, let's not pretend this is the only book written about leadership and teams. There are numerous books out there that range from being worthless to invaluable in helping leaders, organisational resilience and sustainability. I'll let you be the judge of where *Never Forget What It's Like To Be A 'C'* fits within these parameters.

The story is based on a chance encounter with a CEO back in 2008, and the subsequent journey we embarked on to understand why his company was failing.

Everything seemed to be in place for his business to succeed. As a global provider of Business Process Services, they were innovators, leaders in their field and at the forefront of technology. So what was wrong?

The story takes us from a meeting that happened by chance, through a series of events that helped a failing organisation and its leadership team understand what was holding them back from becoming a successful global player.

Yes, there is a single key factor that stifles success, but one has to recognise that many things influence this factor. By focusing on this one factor, it will instantly have a major impact on what is holding you back from being successful as a leader and as an organisation.

"Enjoy your search for TFF: The Forgotten Factor."

A CHANCE MEETING

It all began back in January 2008. I was spending yet another week based in a hotel in Birmingham working with one of our clients on a long-term change programme. The evenings were usually spent with my laptop open, researching and developing our latest project, and a meal provided by room service.

This particular Tuesday evening was different, though; and later, on reflection, here was a lesson: any slight change to the status quo can create real opportunity.

An eagerly awaited FA Cup third round replay was on the cards and, although my team was taking on the giants of Premiership football, anticipation was high, having drawn the previous encounter at home. I remember the night well as it was very rare for a lowly team to get an airing on TV, and with no sports channels provided in the hotel bedrooms, I was off to the bar to enjoy the match in the company of like-minded followers.

Finding a seat in the lounge with a view of the screen proved a challenge, but I finally found a seat at a table with three other people who, it transpired, were due to attend a business conference the following day. After brief introductions we settled down to watch the match.

Forty-five minutes sitting on the edge of our seats, and into first-half added time, the deadlock was broken; my team was going into half time a goal down.

Things didn't get any better and 12 minutes into the second half, two more opposition goals, we were three down with no way back. This was the turning point in the evening and the catalyst for how the conversation changed from football to more pressing matters for the three other occupants at our table.

It wasn't my intention to listen in to the unfolding situation, but with my interest in the football waning, my attention was caught by the open conversation happening around me.

"Well, let's just hope we get some inspiration tomorrow," Brian was saying. "Things have got to change."

"It's all very well saying things have got to change, but if we don't know what it is that needs to change, what do you suggest we do?" asked Joe.

"We need to find out which area is under-performing to start with. I have a feeling that it could be an operations problem. We can start with your area – what do you think, Joe? You're the Operations Director, after all," came the reply.

"That's easy to say, Brian, but I don't think it's just one area that has an issue. There seems to be a variety of different areas that are just not pulling their weight. It's all too easy to pick on operations. Whilst you were overseas I've spent a considerable amount of time with the Exec Team developing our strategy, but for some reason it's just not working."

Leslie was looking exasperated. "Come on you two, this is getting us nowhere. What we need to establish is how you propose we identify where the problem lies."

This started me thinking. Before being able to tackle a problem within an organisation, one has to recognise its very existence. This team was already into the first of a series of stages to resolving their problem. Obvious, I know, but often a problem will have an impact some considerable time before it is recognised and ultimately brought to the attention of someone who can do something about it.

I wanted to congratulate the team on recognising the first step and explain that when there appears to be a broad organisational issue, they will need to follow a clear process. I had in mind what I called the 'six plus three' basic steps to get their organisation on track to becoming successful:

1. **Recognise the very existence of the problem**
2. **Understand the problem**
3. **Know your organisation well enough to be able to understand the areas where the problem exists**
4. **Establish what the situation would be like if the problem didn't exist**
5. **Establish the shortfalls**
6. **Develop a leadership plan to achieve step 4**
7. **Implement the plan**
8. **Monitor and evaluate progress**
9. **Recognise, communicate success**

It occurred to me that they were trying to get to step 5 before really understanding what the problem was.

Leslie continued: "I partly agree with Joe here – we have developed a great strategy in sales but nothing's changed; in fact, sometimes I think we're going backwards instead of making progress."

"Backwards? It's ridiculous, we'll be out of business within 18 months at this rate instead of being global leaders. We have the right product, the right route to market and the best marketing team brought in from our competitors.

After tomorrow I'm going to lock myself away and try to work out where we are going wrong. Whilst I'm doing that, I suggest you both get your people working harder to get a grip on things. I'll tell the rest of the exec the same."

Joe and Leslie glanced at each other. "It's getting late and I need to pull this month's sales report together," muttered Leslie.

"I'll meet you both in reception at 8.30 in the morning – that should give us enough time to get to the conference. Goodnight both."

"Goodnight, Leslie."

"Goodnight Les. I must turn in too, Brian. I just want to cast my eye over the operations strategy again – see if we're missing something – but I'm sure it's not my area that's the problem."

"Okay, goodnight Joe, I'll see you in the morning."

The match – remember that game of football? – was now over with a 5–0 drubbing, but seemed relatively insignificant in contrast to the conversation that I had overheard. It was playing on my mind as I finished the last of my drink before turning in.

Brian was still sitting there looking glum and must have sensed I was about to leave. "I'm sorry about that," he said, "I guess you picked the wrong table to sit at to watch the game tonight."

"That's fine," I replied. "I couldn't help but overhear some of your conversation. It sounds like you're having a bit of a problem but just can't put your finger on what it is. I hope you get it sorted out soon and things start to improve for you."

"Thanks, let's hope so – but I am at a loss right now as to where I'm going wrong. I thought I had the best team around me, but now I'm not so sure."

This was interesting. Was Brian challenging his own ability to recruit the right leadership team, I wondered? "I know this is none of my business, Brian, but what makes you say that?" I heard myself asking him. Brian went quiet, deep in thought. Perhaps I shouldn't have asked the question – after all, we didn't know each other, so why would he open up to me?

"That's a good question," he said finally. "I wish I knew the answer to that one."

"Well, you seem to have some doubts – maybe you should look at what is giving you those doubts."

"That's easy to say, but I'm struggling to put my finger on it. Maybe the conference tomorrow will help give me some direction. All I know is that business is nowhere near as good as it should be, things have to change, and change quickly."

"It sounds like there's a lot riding on this conference tomorrow – what's it about?"

Brian pulled a small leaflet from his inside jacket pocket and handed it to me. "Here you are, these are the details."

It was titled Business Analysis for Organisational Success, showing the conference details and speakers.

"This looks interesting, but why do you believe this conference will help to solve your problems?" I asked.

"All I know is we need to change and quickly. One of the sessions is about reshaping an organisation; hopefully we will get a better understanding of what needs to be done to get my company in the right shape so that it has a future," said a troubled Brian.

It was getting late and tomorrow was going to be a long day. It was time to bid my farewells and get some much-needed sleep.

"Brian, I'd love to spend more time with you tonight, but I have a long, tough day with a client tomorrow and need to turn in now. I hope you have a great day tomorrow and you get the answers you are looking for."

Brian stood. "Me too. I enjoyed your questions – it's got me thinking. Thanks and goodnight."

"And goodnight to you, too." I reached into my top pocket, pulled out a business card and handed it to Brian. "I was just thinking, where are you based?" I asked.

"We're in central London," he replied.

"Well look, if tomorrow doesn't turn out as expected, feel free to call me. I may well have some more questions for you!"

And that was a chance meeting.

I went to bed wondering if I would hear from Brian in the future, or whether his conference would provide him with the answers he was desperately looking for.

Brian went to bed believing tomorrow would be the turning point for him, and his business would start to deliver everything he expected it to.

"How can you ever fix a problem that you don't even recognise exists?"

A MEETING NOT BY CHANCE

More than two weeks had gone by since the chance meeting – the conversation I had overheard Brian having with two of his exec team – and the subsequent chat I had had with Brian had been almost forgotten. I was having some success working with a medium-sized organisation that had been experiencing some difficulty in creating an aligned leadership team, and I became absorbed in their dilemma and ensuing progress.

Positive developments had been made over the months we worked together. Small changes at first, followed by great leaps forward as the team started to enjoy success, and individually they were more prepared to take some calculated risks within the parameters they had agreed. The Managing Director was starting to let go and trust his team to make decisions.

With some sadness, but great delight, it was time to let this organisation go. The senior team was stronger and well placed to continue moving their business forward. To coin an old cliché, my work there was done.

A few days later I was at Heathrow Airport waiting for a flight to Copenhagen. I had been invited to speak at a conference the following day for a major Danish travel organisation on 'Power relationships, politics and ambiguity, and the impact on leadership'. I was using the pre-boarding time to put the finishing touches to my speech when my mobile phone rang.

Not recognising the caller number, I was in two minds as to whether to answer the call or not; after all, the departure lounge at Heathrow wasn't the quietest place to take a call, but something was telling me to take the call anyway.

Having spent too much time deliberating, my voicemail clicked in. "Thank you for calling. Unfortunately, I am unable to take your call right now. Please leave me your name, number and a short message and I will get back to you as soon as I possibly can." (I really must change that message soon!) Whoever called had left me a message.

My theory is that if someone leaves a message, then they want to talk with me. Speculative sales calls aside, there is always the question of whether it is a potential new client calling. I dialled in to my voicemail.

"Hi, this is Brian Jeffers" – the name wasn't ringing any bells – "we met in a Birmingham hotel a few weeks ago. We were watching a game of football" – it was all coming back to me – "and we ended the evening having an interesting conversation." So we did. "You asked me some challenging questions, which got me thinking. As you gave me your business card, I was just wondering if we could get together at some stage. You've now got my number from this phone call. Please call me and perhaps we can arrange to meet. Thanks and hopefully we can catch up soon. Cheers, Brian."

Okay, here was the CEO of a global provider of Business Process Services, who was having some issues with growing his business. As I remember, it seemed worse than that; his company was getting close to becoming non-existent. So I called him back straight away.

"Hello, Brian Jeffers here."

"Brian, hi, I got your message. Sorry I missed you but I'm in the departure lounge at Heathrow and it's somewhat noisy here."

"Hey, that's no problem, thanks for calling back so quickly. Look, I enjoyed our chat in Birmingham and would like to bounce a few thoughts around with you, if you're interested."

"Absolutely, I'm just on my way to Copenhagen for a conference and will be back on Thursday. If I remember correctly your offices are somewhere in central London. I have a clear diary for Friday, so how about we meet up late morning?"

"That sounds good for me, but I would rather meet off-site if possible. Let me buy you some lunch, I know of just the place not too far from my offices if that works for you."

Our gate had been called. "That's a deal Brian, I have to catch a plane now. Can you email me the details please? My address is on my business card."

"Will do and thanks," Brian said. "Enjoy your conference and I hope you get plenty from it. I'm looking forward to seeing you on Friday."

"Thanks. See you then." It was abundantly clear that he had no idea I was the keynote speaker at the event.

Making my way to the jet bridge I returned to thinking about the impending conference speech, although in the back of my mind was the brief conversation I had just had with Brian Jeffers, CEO of a major global player who was in need of help. I remembered his exec team was already at the first stage of resolving their problem – they recognised they had a problem. It occurred to me that maybe they needed some extra help to get to the second stage – to understand the problem – and some support through it.

The speech in Denmark seemed to go well and before I knew it I was back at the airport waiting for my flight back home. On the plane back to London I got round to thinking about the next day's meeting with Brian. He had emailed me the name and address of the restaurant where we were meeting and I started to wonder how he was going to understand what the problem was. I had an idea, but I needed to ask Brian some searching questions first.

The following lunchtime I met Brian as planned. The restaurant was ideal. It was busy, yet somehow offered a degree of privacy. He was already seated at our table reading the menu.

"Thanks for coming," he said, as he stood and shook my hand. "Please, take a seat."

"It's good to see you again Brian. What a great choice of restaurant," I said.

"I've become somewhat of a regular here over the last 12 months; it's one of those places where I find I can think better. How was Denmark?"

"It was just fine, albeit a tiring trip," I replied. "I'm intrigued, but let's order first."

After ordering, Brian asked me about Denmark and what the attraction was in travelling there for a conference. "Ah, a good question," I replied. "Actually I was invited there to make a speech at a company conference. It's something I'm being asked to do more and more."

He looked slightly embarrassed at his original assumption and smiled.

"That explains the fleeting visit. What was your speech about, if you don't mind me asking?"

It was my turn to look slightly embarrassed. "Well, the theme of the conference was 'Power relationships, politics and ambiguity, and the impact on leadership'.

Not the most scintillating subject, I know, but someone had to speak about it!"

We both laughed and started to relax more. As our drinks arrived, I took the opportunity to change the conversation. "As I recall, you were going to a conference yourself when we met in Birmingham," I said. "How did you get on?"

"Well," he began, "it was interesting in parts and I thought that we had gained some useful ideas about how we could become more successful."

"That's encouraging," I said not wanting to push him too hard right now. But Brian seemed to look beyond me, as if he was trying to figure out what to say next. I decided to help. "What did you find most interesting?" I asked.

"There were a couple of sessions that I felt were useful; first, there was a discussion about Continuous Operational Improvement – I thought there was some merit in the key observations and messages from the host."

"Okay," I interrupted, "what messages have you found helpful in developing your business?"

Brian looked bemused. "What I took from it was that in today's global economy, instead of thinking strategically, a good proportion of companies are just reacting to global demands. While I accept that is one way to deal with change, maybe a much more effective approach is to systematically integrate the business analysis discipline throughout the whole organisation, right from strategy to actual implementation, and ensure that it is integrated across multiple roles."

"That makes sense to me; what else interested you?" "The final session was called 'Improving your Ability to Adapt'. The presenter stressed that adaptability is not just a nice-to-have competency or behaviour, but an absolute must-have. She went on to say that it can be a competitive advantage for you, as a leader of your organisation and for your organisation in its market place."

"Wow, it sounds like you gained some valuable insights," I commented, although in the back of my mind I knew there were some underlying issues still.

As our food arrived we settled into sharing general views about being a key player in an ever-changing global market.

"Perhaps there's something to be said for 'Moore's Law' then," I suggested.

"Is that the view that since the 1960s, in building computer hardware, the number of transistors used in an integrated circuit doubles every two years?" he asked.

"That's the one," I said, "and research suggests that the exponential improvement has dramatically enhanced technological and social change, productivity and economic growth over the last 50-odd years."

Brian thought about this and then said, "I can't see that continuing for another 50 years, though."

"Probably not, but it must be the same in your business; you need to keep innovating and moving forward, maybe consider Moore's Law a little more."

"You have a point," he said.

"The food is great, a real good find," I said. "hopefully you will allow me the opportunity to repay your hospitality one day."

Brian smiled and, placing his knife and fork on his empty plate, said "Oh, I'm sure you will have that opportunity."

"Excellent, now perhaps you can tell me what's really going on with your company. When we met in Birmingham I did say I might have some more questions for you. It seems maybe the conference didn't deliver for you. So what's the problem?"

In a way Brian looked relieved. "To tell you the truth things have not improved. I know we have a problem, but I just cannot put a finger on what it is. I came back from the conference with some ideas and told my team to get on and implement some of the ideas I had."

"So what's the problem?" I asked, almost pre-empting the answer I was about to get.

"That's the problem," he replied, "I don't know what the problem is. Sounds crazy, doesn't it!"

"Welcome to step two," I congratulated him.

The CEO looked puzzled. "What do you mean by step two? Step two of what? I'm confused now."

Smiling, I said: "Look Brian, you will never solve a problem until you know what the problem is. You have achieved step one by recognising that a problem exists. Now you need to work out what the problem is."

"Slow down there, I know what the problem is – we are not a successful business. We have all the right innovations, the right people and the right opportunities but we are losing money. That's the problem."

"That's not the problem, that's the result, the output of it. The problem you have is what is causing that result. Step two, my friend."

"Hmm," Brian reflected on this last comment. "I think I'm beginning to understand, but how on earth do I find out what the problem is, then? I don't know where to begin."

From what I had heard thus far, I knew I could help.

I saw a way to get Brian and his company back on track. I could help them identify the real problem, but it would need commitment from the whole leadership team.

"So what prompted your call to me on Tuesday, then? It sounds like you have taken a few ideas from the conference. How is that helping?" I asked.

"Nothing has changed at all. Everyone is working flat out, I have started to walk about the offices when I'm there and it's very apparent that the majority of the staff are really busy. There appears to be a high level of energy about the place and a fun atmosphere. I was surprised at that, given what I am expecting from people and the demands I am putting on them."

He went on, "I don't want to lose my good people, and I need them if we are ever to get through this successfully. I'm frightened that the increased pressure from me will ruin the atmosphere for them. That would be the final nail in the coffin. Does that make sense?"

I nodded warmly. "That makes perfect sense to me." "I liked the chat we had in Birmingham and, well, I called because you came across as someone who may be able to help. I had a look at your website and you have been involved in some key projects recently with some seemingly impressive results!"

"Okay, you found me out," I replied, rather diffidently. "I may be able to help you with step two and possibly step three also. For me to help, though, I will need something from you."

Brian interrupted: "Look, naturally I'm prepared to pay for any time you spend with us."

Holding my hand up, I said "That's not what I'm thinking about right now. We can talk about my fees later.

Tell me, how many people have you got in your exec team and how many direct reports do they have?"

Looking a bit puzzled, he replied "I have five directors who report straight to me: that's Joe, he's the Operations Director – you met him in Birmingham with Leslie, our Sales and Marketing Director. I am still thinking about splitting that role and bringing in a professional marketer to head up that side of it."

"Okay, that's the three of you I met. Who are the other three?"

"Then there's our Finance Director, Malik," he continued. "He's also responsible for purchasing. The final two are James and Mary. James is Technical Director – R&D comes under his remit also; and finally, Mary is HR Director with a broader responsibility for the admin staff as well."

"And their direct reports?"

"Let me see, Joe has four managers reporting in to him right now, Malik has two managers, James and Mary both have three managers each and Leslie currently has four managers – three in sales and one in marketing. That's the full leadership team."

Adding the team up as we went along, I said: "I make that 22 people in total, including you, Brian. Is that right?"

"That's it right now. It may change in the near future, but I guess that will depend on the possible new marketing role."

"Thanks Brian. Okay, if I am to help, what I need from you and your whole leadership team is commitment to spend one day together with me – that's all. I want their commitment, along with yours, to get involved on the day, no-holds-barred and on an equal playing field.

No hierarchy for the day. That's it, that's what I need from you. How does that sound?"

"That's easy enough to arrange," he replied. "But why the whole leadership team? Surely this is an issue that the exec team should be sorting out?"

"I understand, it's a big ask to take all of your leadership team out for a whole day, but if we are going to get to the root of the problem, that's the commitment I need from you."

"But the whole team at once?" he argued. "It's impossible, I need some managers there to keep things moving along."

I was ready for this. "Just this once, the whole team Brian; nothing less, that's the deal, that's the commitment I need from you."

"But…" he began, "why can't we have two sessions and mix the teams up? That would help the business out by having some managers there all the time."

"It's all or nothing," I said forcefully. I needed him to be very clear about my wish. "Let me explain. There is one key factor that often stifles success, and is probably stifling your success. By focusing on this one factor, it will instantly have a major impact on what is holding you and your leadership team back from being successful as leaders and as an organisation. I want you all to recognise this together. No exceptions, that's it."

"Surely then if it's only one thing that's holding us back, why not just tell me what it is and we can get on with building a successful business?" Brian continued to argue. "It's not that simple," I replied. "I wish it was. I need your whole team to have, and share, an experience, the messages from which will last the rest of your, and their, leadership careers. You've seen the results on my website regarding my work. The same is available to you – just trust me and commit one day with me, that's all."

He pondered on this for a few moments. "Right," he said, "let me talk with the exec team and let you know. Is that okay?"

I didn't want him to lose this opportunity, and I knew that once he got back to his business, the moment, and the right decision were gone, so I said, "Two weeks today I am free – let's put it in our diaries for then."

He looked at me blankly, so I went on: "You organise your people to be away from the business for the whole day – all 21 of them plus you. I will organise a suitable venue. I know what I need from them and they know how I work. How does that sound?"

"If I agree," he said holding his hands up in near-defeat, "how much will this cost me?"

"Aha, back to the cost," I teased, "here's what I am prepared to do. I have asked for a sizeable commitment from you in terms of time and your leadership team. Here's my commitment to you: pay only for the venue hire and refreshments – pay me nothing for the day."

"What – nothing at all?"

"That's what I said, nothing for the day; however, after our day together, consider the value for you, your people and your business, and you decide what it was worth."

I had his interest, so I continued: "If you decide the day was of no value, Brian, pay me nothing at all and I'll walk away with no ill feeling. However, if it has got you through step two and step three, you decide the worth in that and pay me accordingly."

"But why, then, would I pay you anything at all, even if we have some success?"

I expected it. "Quite simply, I trust you, Brian. You need help; I believe I can help you and I want you to trust me to deliver what I believe I can deliver."

"Wow, that's some belief you have there – you really do believe in your ability to help a failing company. It looks like we have a deal," he said, with a grin on his face. "It feels like a great weight has been lifted already."

With that, we shook hands and agreed to speak on the phone the following week to finalise the details for the day. Brian paid for lunch, gave me his contact details and we went our separate ways shortly after.

I couldn't help thinking on the way home that in two weeks' time, 22 people would be having an enlightening time with a realisation that there is one key factor that is hindering their success – their whole future.

Brian returned to his office motivated by the thought of getting to grips with his problem. He called an immediate exec meeting to explain what would be happening in two weeks' time and to gain the commitment from his people. The following week consisted of a combination of client meetings, research into the concept of Resilient Leadership and some much-needed family time.

On the Wednesday I put in a call to Brian to confirm details about our day together on Friday week.

"Thanks for calling," he said, on answering his mobile. "We are all set here. I had some difficulties getting the whole team to commit, but I have been assured that they will all be there."

"That's good news Brian, I knew you would get it sorted out," I replied. "I've arranged a room in the centre of London. They know me there and know the type of room I need. I'll email you the address."

"That's fine. What time are you suggesting we start? I need to let everyone know."

"My suggestion is 9.30 for a coffee and some introductions, then we can really get going by 10 if that's okay with you."

"No problem," Brian replied, "I'll make sure we are all there ready for 9.30."

"Oh, and one more thing; just to remind you, we are all equal on the day so I suggest that everyone should dress casually. I want to make sure that there is absolutely no business attire at all. Is that clear?"

"It's sounding more like a holiday that anything else," he laughed. "I'll make sure everyone knows. Anything else we need to know or bring?"

"Nope, that's it. Just 22 committed people with open minds. I'll bring the rest."

"Fine, see you on Friday next week then," and Brian was gone.

So there we were. Everything was set to get to step two and hopefully achieve step three. I had work to do in preparation, and little time to do it.

"How can we solve a problem we don't talk about?"

SETTING UP THE 'GAME'

At the beginning of the following week I ran through what I needed for Friday and the day with Brian Jeffers and his team. All I needed was a pack of special cards and I would be ready.

I first came across the game several years earlier. It was in a fairly raw state then, but worked well up to a point. It was then that I realised why some leaders fail, and, ultimately, the organisation they work for fails, too.

Over the next three years I played the game on many occasions at all different levels in organisations, ranging from SMEs to multi-global businesses, and in both the public and private sectors. Each time I learned from the outcomes and modified the game for the next event.

It was time to get a final set of cards produced for Friday, so I called my printers and explained what I needed. They promised everything would be ready and delivered to me by Thursday afternoon.

Tuesday and Wednesday involved a trip to Düsseldorf for a final planning and design meeting with a client looking to change the way they approached their specific market. We established real clarity about where they were going and how to get there.

Flying back to London on Wednesday night, and feeling pleased with a successful two days, it was time now to concentrate on Brian Jeffers and his problem. Thursday would be spent getting everything in place for the following day and, providing the printers had completed their side of it, there was little left to do.

Friday was going to be an interesting day. I only hoped that Brian had managed to fulfil his commitment and get all of his people to the venue, and on time.

The printers couriered a small parcel to my office that arrived on Thursday morning. I checked the parcel and smiled with satisfaction. Perfect – I have everything I need for tomorrow. It promises to be a thought-provoking and rewarding day, I realised.

On Friday morning I picked up the game and headed for the venue. I arrived shortly before 9.00 and, not surprisingly, I was the first there. Good, I had time to set things up before anyone else appeared.

THE 'GAME'

So let me explain a bit about how it works. In its simplest form, the game is designed to replicate a simple organisational hierarchy, either in its totality or as an area of business within the organisation.

The structure is basic, comprising only three levels: A, B and C. These levels can also be interpreted as roles in an organisation. For example, in a small organisation:
- Level A could be identified as the CEO, MD or possibly the proprietor
- Level B would represent the management team
- Level C would therefore be recognised as the workforce

In a larger organisation:
- Level A could be identified as a member of the exec team or the senior management team
- Level B would represent the management team or second-line management
- Level C would therefore be recognised as first-line management or supervisory level

The first important point to recognise here is that these levels are representative of a role or job in a structure; they are not representing an individual person. In the early days of playing this game, feedback during the game quickly became personal, about the individual in that role and not about the role itself. This game is about highlighting activity within a role or at a level in an organisational structure.

Based around achieving one clear objective, it explores how organisations and individual teams within an organisation communicate to achieve the objective. What could be easier, I hear you asking yourself?

The answer is nothing, except that humans are involved in the process. Having now played the game more than 200 times at various levels and in completely different markets, one thing is evident: once humans are involved, the simplest of tasks become complicated, cumbersome and destined for disaster. The game will demonstrate how and why this occurs although, in itself, that's not enough. Understanding what to do about it is more important.

Playing this game exposes our fundamental weaknesses as people and identifies what we can do as leaders, and organisations, to overcome these weaknesses.

The standard set-up to play the game is to have one person take the role of level A and two people become level B managers/leaders. The rest of the group make up the C population.

THE A

Through experience, this is a tough position and is often open to early criticism during the review and feedback session. For this reason, it is important that the person who takes on this role has the capacity to handle the criticism in the right way. It is imperative to remind everyone that this is about the role and not the person representing that role.

Although I never explain to the group that each level represents a basic organisational hierarchy, very quickly the group identifies A as the senior person in the game, and it doesn't take long before they start to look towards this level for some direction.

The A will have an objective to achieve that the Bs and Cs are not initially aware of.

THE B

This level, on the surface, probably works the hardest. During the review and feedback session, the Bs will start to be blamed for the lack of performance and, owing to their position, will receive criticism from both the A and the Cs. It is easy to lay the blame here, but is this about blame? Obviously not, I hear you saying. Play the game and watch it unfold.

The Bs struggle, they will become overworked and we'll explore why this happens as the game develops. The Bs will see themselves as managers, working for A and managing a team of Cs. Maybe this is where the problem lies. Time will tell.

The Bs start the game with nothing more than the introduction briefing and the constraints within which they can play the game.

THE C

The workforce. This group of people see themselves as the workers, they behave like workers and become extremely productive. The issue here is: What are they productive at? They look up to their Bs and the A, and expect some direction from their superiors. The big question has to be: How long can they stay focused on achievement?

The C population are organised subliminally to work in units/teams and assume the role of workers for the B they believe is their manager.

The Cs have information. This is the only level where data (in the form of cards) is allocated. How it is used is varied from game to game, and we'll explore this in the review/feedback session.

THE SET-UP

Before Brian and his leadership team arrived, I needed to set up the information for the Cs and organise the seating in the main room. Both of these elements are fundamental to maximise participant involvement and, ultimately, their learning.

THE SEATING

This is the way I set up the seating for Brian. With 22 people, I decided to work with one A, three Bs and 18 Cs. This would ensure that the game replicated workable team sizes. To bring in as many facets as possible, I divided the Cs into three different-sized groups. The first group comprised five Cs, the second group six Cs and the final group eight Cs. Before you castigate me for having more Cs than people, there is a reason for this and it will be explained later.

The seating plan opposite highlights the position for each participant and indicates the direction in which they are facing at the start of the game. This arrangement is quite deliberate and designed to bring out the maximum number of messages during the activity.

Never Forget What It's Like To Be A 'C'

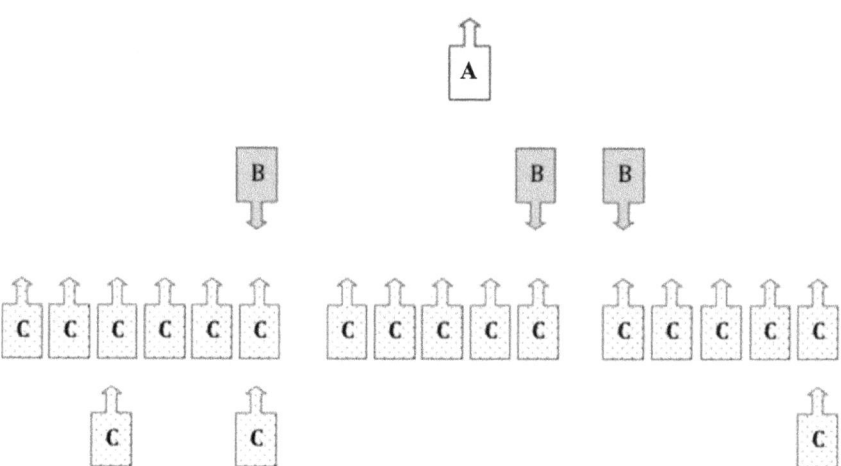

Two more things needed to be done before Brian and his team arrived. First, I placed a pack of self-adhesive, repositionable notes (Post-it® Notes)* on each chair with the exception of one C chair that was left empty. It didn't really matter which chair was left empty; the learning is exactly the same regardless of which chair it is. To aid the review and feedback session, I used packs of blue notes for the A, green notes for the Bs and yellow notes for the Cs.

The final task was to organise the information for each C. I mentioned earlier that the C level was the only level that was given data. The data is simply a few cards for each C. The individual cards have a basic image on them and there are eight different images in total. For the game to work, there needed to be sufficient cards of each image for all the Cs to have one card of each image. In this case, I had each image produced 20 times to ensure that there were sufficient to complete the task.

The way the cards are organised is important. They have to be arranged so that all the Cs have only one image (card) in common, that is, one card is identical across all the Cs, all the other images (cards) will have at least one C not having that image in their pack.

I organised 18 packs for the Cs with seven or eight cards in each pack and I chose the picture of a musical bar note symbol as the common image (card).

As there would be 18 of the musical bar note symbol, I also doubled up on the other symbols with different Cs to ensure that there were 18 of each symbol used in total. I made certain that no other symbol was replicated across all the Cs.

To add a small red herring, I also included in one of the packs a card with the image of a winner's cup. Often the C who had this card assumed it was the answer to the task.

There are many other variations and nuances that could be introduced to make the challenge more difficult, but experience tells me that the simpler the game is kept, the greater the learning gained from playing it.

That was it – the game was ready and, as if on cue, Brian walked in. "Good morning," he said.

"Ah, good morning Brian, I'm all set here so let's go and find a coffee while the rest of your people arrive," I said. "I've organised a private room where we can take refreshments, so I'll remind reception to point everyone in that direction as they arrive."

"Good idea, they should all be here by 9.30," he smiled, looking at his watch. With that, we headed for the coffee. "I'm pleased you've arrived a bit early," I said. I want to make sure we are clear about the day ahead. I would like you to open the event with a few words about the day in general terms. We can do this in the coffee area, if that's okay with you. I would also like you to close the day. Apart from these two occasions, I need you to be a willing participant with your team. How does that sound?"

"Absolutely fine with me. Is there anything specific you want me to say?"

I looked at Brian. "Yes, there is, as a matter of fact. I would like you to explain why we are all here and why it was so important that the whole team attended together. I also want you to make it clear that we are all equal today and, as such, there is no hierarchy during the event. I realise some people, and this may include you, Brian, may find this difficult to adhere to, but it is important," I said.

He looked puzzled. "Why is it so important?" he asked.

"Let me explain. It has long been recognised that the flattest organisational structure helps elevate an employee's level of responsibility in the organisation. We need everyone to take some responsibility today." I went on: "By removing the layers of management, today will improve the coordination and speed of communication between employees and, therefore, with the finite amount of time we have available, we need everyone to be able to communicate freely and quickly."

"That makes some sense. I'm sure the team will be fine," the CEO replied.

"Good. For today to be successful, we need people to be open, to be themselves without fear of any recrimination or repercussions." I carried on: "Just be you, but without the badge of authority today; it will be a valuable experience for you and all your people, I promise."

I had another request. "I need you and the exec team to do something for me," I said.

"Go on," he said.

"When we all go into the other room, I would like you and the exec to sit on seats that are part of a group of seats, not in the top four seats. It will become obvious what I mean when we get there. Can you quietly let the other five know, please?" I asked.

"This sounds intriguing. I hope you're not planning to embarrass any of us," Brian said, "I'll discreetly let them know."

"Thanks, no embarrassing moments, I assure you," I said, trying to reassure him. "I would like as many of you as possible to experience things from a different perspective, and the seating is important for this to happen."

His team had started to arrive, so it was time to get to know today's participants. "One final thing, Brian," I said, before we moved on to be introduced to some of the arrivals, "as we go through the day, I would like you to think about some of the behaviours you observe in the team. You never know – there may be something you see on reflection that triggers a key message for you to close the day with."

He smiled again. "That's what we're here for. Let me introduce you to some of the team," and with that, he guided me towards a group of people. The day had begun.

"The way to succeed is not a secret. It comes about by good preparation, dedication to hard work and ultimately learning from failure."

PLAYING THE 'GAME'

With the introductions over and the CEO's opening address delivered, it was time for me to take over; but before playing the game, it was important to make sure that the group had some element of trust in me as a newcomer to their team. And that's how I saw it; I was a part of their team, working with them, so I needed them to feel the same.

Without going into too much detail – after all, this book is more about the message from playing a game than developing trust – we spent some time talking about how they were feeling at that point in time. With a newcomer to their team, I expected a mixed reaction. This gave me a clue as to how well the organisation communicated internally.

The team had the opportunity to explain why they were there, which again gave me some indication of how effectively they communicated as an organisation. I then wanted to know what they expected/wanted to get out of the day as individuals, and as a management team. Finally, to ensure I could manage their expectations, I asked them to tell me what they expected from me as a team member for the day.

With the introductions over, the team was starting to relax. The CEO was playing his part and fitting in well as an equal to the rest of the team, and they seemed to be accepting him as 'one of them'. It was time to move into the room I had set up earlier for the game to be played in.

I announced that we were now moving to another room and that the only thing they needed to take with them was something to write with; everything else would be safely locked in the private room we were leaving.

Before we entered the new room, I briefed the team. "You may sit on any of the chairs that has a pack of Post-it® Notes on it. Any chair without a pack of notes must remain empty. Is that clear?"

With a few nods and murmurs of agreement, we filed into the room. I helped steer Brian and his directors to some of the empty chairs allocated for the C population. The last thing we needed was for the directors to take up the A or B positions.

With everyone seated, and some looking around in bewilderment, there was one chair not occupied. Perfect, I thought. It was now time to expose a new team to the game. It was time to brief them on the main event of the day. "Okay," I began, "over the next 25 minutes you will be challenged to achieve a simple task. The task is very clear and very achievable, but there are a few constraints that you will have to work within." And I started to explain a few basic rules for the game.

"First and foremost, and this will be more difficult for some than others, the game is to be played in total silence. That means there is to be no vocal communication between you. In fact, the only way you can communicate with each other is through the written form. You all have a pack of notes and something to write with, so this is your method of communication." The usual banter ensued whilst the group came to terms with this first constraint. "Now, let's depersonalise things a bit," I said and moved to the person sitting on the chair I had designated to the A role. "This game is not about individual people," I went on, "but about individual roles in an organisation, so to remove any reference to you personally, I would like you to be referred to as A for the duration of the game and the review/feedback session. Is that okay with you?"

"That's fine with me," replied Chris. Chris Maloney, I had ascertained during our introductions, was head of Client Services and oversaw the customer experience. He was responsible for a small team that had been introduced to ensure that the organisation remained customer-centric throughout its operation. It was apparent that Chris was a strong individual and well respected throughout his peer group. I couldn't see any issues with Chris being the A.

"Good," I replied.

I moved on to the row of three chairs. "We have our A," I said, and in a rather joking way, "so what does that make us?"

A resounding "We are three Bs," and a bit more banter followed.

I carried on: "We now have an A, and three Bs, so what does that make the rest of us in the room?"

"We are all Cs," came the reply.

"Great! We have an A, three Bs and 18 Cs. There are a few more rules, so let me explain them."

"Rule 1 – A, you are only allowed to communicate directly with the three Bs. If for any reason you want to communicate with any of the C population, you will need to do it through a B. Is that clear?"

There were some nods of the head from the group, followed by words of acknowledgement, so I continued.

"Rule 2 – Bs, you are free to communicate directly with anyone in the room except me."

"Rule 3 – Cs, you can communicate directly with anyone in the room with the exception of A (and of course me). If for any reason you need to communicate with A, you will need to do this through one of the three Bs. Are there any questions?"

After a few questions to clarify the rules, I had one last rule to give the group.

"Finally, if you receive a message and you think it needs to be passed on to another position in the room, you must rewrite the message. You cannot just hand the note to someone else; you must rewrite it and pass the new note to the position you want it to go to. "Please just drop the read notes on the floor when you have finished with them. I may collect a few during the game to use in the review session. Are there any final questions?" I asked.

"You said there was a task to achieve. We don't know what the task is," challenged one of the Cs.

"That's a good question. I'm sure the task will become apparent as the game progresses. Any more questions?"

"I don't understand," the C continued. "It's not clear what we are meant to do here," she said.

"You will get to know what the task is," I replied, without wanting to discuss the matter any further.

For some of the group this was fine; they didn't need to know what the task was. For a few, it was less easy to accept – they were clearly puzzled and needed some direction here.

I didn't want to dwell on this right now – it was a point for the review and feedback session – so I simply said "Okay, the game is about to commence. When I say you may begin writing notes, your 25 minutes will start and there is to be no more vocal communication. You may begin writing notes!"

With 22 people looking extremely puzzled and the predictable vocal comments, I reminded them that the next 25 minutes was to be in total silence, and the inevitable learning ensued.

As I started to hand a pre-prepared pack of cards to each of the Cs – with the exception of one C chosen at random whom I missed out – the group tentatively started to write messages to each other, and by the time I had handed the packs of cards out, there was a real buzz in the room. Again, the reason for not handing a pack of cards to one of the Cs will become apparent in the feedback and review session. I placed the spare pack on the empty chair.

I then moved on to the Bs, who were curious about the cards I had been handing out, and gave each of them a card that summarised the rules of the game.

Finally, I handed the A a card that summarised the rules of the game and, in addition, the card had a task for the A to achieve included at the bottom. We were now less than two minutes into the game and things were moving along nicely.

The Cs were writing messages to each other and to the Bs, and there was a real energy in the room, although for all intents and purposes they didn't have a task to achieve. The Bs were becoming more busy as they started to receive messages from their Cs and from the A. They started to deal with the pressure of receiving and replying to messages in very different ways.

Five minutes into the game and the A was becoming more agitated. Remember from the seating layout the A, who was facing away from the rest of the group, could hear plenty of activity going on behind and could feel people getting up and moving around the room, but had little idea about what was actually happening. In fact, there were periodic bouts of laughter emanating from the Cs, which caused the Bs to try and find out what was causing it.

And so the game moved on. A finally realised that the task was on his card and promptly wrote a message to the nearest B (let's call this person B2), explaining what he wanted done. "Please find out what symbols the Cs have," he wrote. B2 was busy responding to messages received from the Cs and immediately put the message from A to the bottom of the pile.

I moved around the room observing the activity and picked up some of the messages that had been discarded. I planned to use these later in the feedback and review session.

"You've had 10 minutes," I announced, "you have 15 minutes left to achieve the task."

With that, the pace of the game picked up. The Cs sent messages to the Bs asking what the task was, and suggesting that A might have a task for them. The Bs complied and asked A what the task was, whilst trying to respond to all the messages they seemed to be receiving. The A was now exasperated. As far as he was concerned, he had given them the task, so he wrote, "I need you to find out the common symbols," and passed the message to B2. Realising that this may not be enough instruction, he then passed a similar message to the other two Bs.

The first B (now referred to as B1) completely ignored the message and carried on responding to the questions being asked by a group of Cs. The other two Bs exchanged glances and one wrote to the other, "What do you think he means?"

"Perhaps it's got something to do with the cards the Cs have," came the reply back.

"Shall we ask them to give us their cards, then?" "Perhaps we could collect them all for A. Maybe that's the task."

"One of my Cs said they should group all the cards." "Okay, let them group them." And so the Bs returned to fielding as many messages as possible.

It became evident that a few of the Cs were starting to lose interest and sat back watching the activity. This is commonplace; after all, we are all very different and react to situations differently. Interestingly enough, the busiest C in the room was the C who didn't have any cards handed to them at the start of the game. This was another observation for the review session.

By now we were 15 minutes into the activity, and little or no progress had been made towards achieving the task. The Cs were forming smaller groups working differently. One group decided that the task was to collect a set of like-minded cards, and consequently set about swapping cards with each other, trying to collect as many of one symbol as possible.

Another group was working on drawing their symbols on Post-it® Notes and passing them to the Bs. A few minutes later the third B (B3), suddenly received a series of notes with different symbols drawn on them.

A third group decided to combine their cards and pass them to a B, suggesting that they should be handed to the A. The 'leader' of this group collected all the cards from this small group and, with a covering note that read, "Please pass to 'A' for us", handed the note and 48 cards to B1. Being somewhat confused, whilst also amused at the gift, B1 read the note and, with a shrug of the shoulders, immediately passed the pack of 48 cards to A.

At this point A had not realised there were cards being circulated; remember, A is facing away from the rest of the group. After shuffling through the cards for a moment, and looking rather confused, A sent a message to B1, who had handed the cards to him, saying "Where did these come from and are there any more?"

"From the Cs and yes," came a quick reply. A realised that perhaps the answer to his task lay within the cards, and gave a new instruction to B1. "Please pass all the cards to me. Ask the other Bs to do the same."

On receiving this instruction, B1 felt in possession of some responsibility now and, not having had any contact with the other Bs until this point in time, passed a message to them that read "Collect all the cards with pictures on and pass them to me."

Not surprisingly, this message was received very differently. B2 was busy responding to messages received from the Cs and left the request unattended. B3 wrote a message and passed it to B1 with one simple word on it, "Why?" After B1 had read the message and dropped it on the floor, I picked it up – more material for the feedback and review session to follow.

Not wanting to relinquish the little authority B1 felt in possession of, a quick message was scribbled, "I got a note from A asking me to collect them all for him."

Some 20 minutes had now elapsed, so I announced, "You've now had 20 minutes, and you have five more minutes remaining to complete the task." This announcement provoked some nervous laughter and launched the A, Bs and some of the Cs into a frenzy of activity, all trying to make sure the task was completed. There was a small group of Cs who, having given their packs of cards to the A, had little else to do except either wait for the time to lapse or embark on more disruption. The final few minutes saw one group of Cs send a message to B3, announcing that they had the answer.

Driven by the C who had the winner's cup, the only card of its type in the whole game, they decided that this was the odd one out and was the solution. "The answer is the Cup!" they wrote.

This message was subsequently rewritten by B3 and passed to A. Looking somewhat relieved, the A started to relax, believing that the task had been completed on time. At this point, B1 had collected nearly all the remaining packs of cards from the Cs and, realising time was of the essence now, passed them to A with a message "Here are the remaining cards. Good luck!"

One final glance around the room before calling time up and it was evident that there was a range of mixed emotions. The first thing I wanted to do, before we dissected what had gone on and explored how individuals and different levels behaved and why, was to explore these emotions with the group.

I quickly prepared a flip chart writing the letter A at the top; I wrote three Bs a third of the way down the flip chart and then wrote Cs below the Bs, leaving enough room for the A and Bs to place their Post-it® Notes in the appropriate places.

"Okay, that's your time up," I announced. "But before we all start talking, I need you to do one more thing. If you can all find a blank Post-it® Note, what I want you to do is on the top half of the note, please write down what you believe the task was. If you don't know, then put a question mark or just indicate that you have no idea. On the bottom of the Post-it® Note, please write down, or draw, what the solution to the task was. Is that clear?"

These instructions caused some nervous laughter and a group of the Cs commented that they had no idea what the answer to either of the instructions was.

I continued: "When you have completed your Post-it® Note, please place it on the flip chart where indicated and return to your seat as quickly as possible."

When everyone had returned to their seats, and before the chattering became too lively, I invited the A to turn his seat around and join the rest of the group.

"Making mistakes provides some of the best lessons we can learn. Our past mistakes become future successes."

LEVEL FEELINGS

"Okay, before we get into what went on over the last 25 minutes, I would like us to explore how we felt during the game. Let's start with the Cs and, in particular, the three Cs who were seated behind the main group of Cs. How did you feel during this game?"

C-LEVEL FEELINGS

The first C said "I felt left out, and completely confused. Was I meant to be doing anything specific?"

"That's a good question," I replied, "and we will discuss it a bit later, but for now I just want to get some words from everyone that describe how you felt. So for you it was confusion and being left out. I see you were at the back completely on your own.

"What about you two?" I indicated to the two Cs who were nearer to each other at the back of the largest group of Cs. "How did you both feel?"

"Well, I felt as though I wasn't a part of what was happening. I was being ignored, no one seemed to want to include me so I started to lose interest."

"So for you it was a feeling of being ignored, not being a part of the activity and a feeling of a lack of interest in the game." I summed up and added a few words to the flip chart. "And for you?" I asked, indicating to the third C at the back, "How did you feel?"

"I felt left out and confused like the other two but I had fun. I had a good time with the Cs in front of me exchanging messages and getting along just fine."

"Yes I noticed, I have some of your messages here – we'll have a look at some of them in a minute, they were very enlightening!" I said, grinning.

Moving along to the next group of Cs, I said: "How about this group of five here? You seemed to be working more closely with the B in front of you. How did you all feel during the game?"

"I felt great," said the first C, "I was near to Sam and…" I interrupted "Let's refer to Sam as B – it's about the role not the person – is that ok?"

"Sorry, yes, I was closest to B and had a lot of messages coming to me, and also managed to get my messages to B quickly. I felt needed and did everything I could to help my B. But the other Cs didn't seem bothered, so I tried to get them more involved."

"But you asked me for my cards," said the next C, "and I didn't know why you wanted them; you just seemed to be trying to take control."

"Again, we will look at this in a while, let's just stick to how you felt about that," I said.

"I felt in the dark – it was like other people knew what was going on but I didn't, and no one told me what was happening."

I added the words 'in the dark' to the flip chart, "and what about the three of you in the group here?" indicating the final three at the end of this group.

"Well, I was happy, I didn't feel under pressure at all. I just thought that someone would ask me for something if they needed it. No one asked me for anything, so I had a chat with the Cs either side of me. There wasn't much else to do."

"Yep, as I didn't know what was happening and no one told me what to do, I chatted, by notes, with the others. I did feel a bit guilty that other people seemed to be doing a lot but I had nothing to do. That guilty feeling soon passed, though, when I got a few messages from the C next to me."

"Hmm, a bit guilty then," the flip chart was filling up. The final C on this side of the room added: "I got bored really quickly. The other side of the room were really busy – they didn't tell us what they were doing and I had no instructions. After about 15 minutes, I couldn't be bothered any more. I just gave up and watched everyone else."

"Thank you for your honesty," I commented, "we will look at why that happened in a few minutes. Let's talk to the Cs on the other side of the room first."

Moving across to the other end of the line of Cs, I posed the same question. Very quickly the C at the far end of the line spoke up: "I felt really isolated, I was the furthest away from the B and nothing was getting through to me. I tried to communicate with the B but my messages just got lost."

"That became really frustrating for me," said the next C. "You kept asking me what was going on and I didn't know, I was as much in the dark as you were. I was trying to get a response from the B, but it just wasn't happening."

I moved on to the next four. "I was nearest the B and we found it easy to communicate. I was getting replies quite quickly to my messages; in fact, we had quite a laugh, to be honest, as there was nothing to do, so we started discussing the weekend and what we were both going to do." That caused a ripple of laughter from the room.

"We may have a look at some of those messages a bit later, but please tell me how you were feeling," I said.

"I felt quite happy and relaxed really, although I was a bit concerned that we didn't seem to be doing anything productive. I thought someone must know what was going on and I would find out sooner or later." Back to the flip chart.

"And what about you two in the middle of this group of Cs?"

"Alright, I suppose." "Just alright?"

"I felt as though I wasn't needed and that other people in the room knew what we were meant to be doing but didn't want to tell us all."

"That's exactly how I felt, so I decided to just let them get on with it. After all, I had some cards and I knew they must be important so someone would come to me eventually to find out what I had. In fact, I found it very easy not to participate – reminds me of work a bit."

"Well, I didn't have any cards at all," the other replied. "I felt quite useless and almost like I wasn't trusted with them at the beginning." More words were added to the flip chart.

That brought a question from the other side of the room, "You didn't have any cards at all?"

"No, not to start with."

"I thought every C had some cards. Did anyone else not have any cards?" No one else declared they had no cards.

I needed to hold this discussion for later, so I moved things along, "Again, this is a good discussion to have but can we hold it for now? I promise we will come back to it. Let's find out how everyone else felt before we explore these points. We've heard from the two end groups of Cs, so let's hear from the group in the middle. How did you all feel?"

"For me, that was a terrible 25 minutes. I felt as if things were out of control; no one seemed to have any idea what we were meant to be doing, and every time I asked B what I could do, I got told to look busy and things would sort themselves out over time."

"That's exactly what I felt like. I tried to get some order installed but the B was too busy to get everyone in line."

"It was a bit different for me. I realised early on what the task was and felt empowered to try and complete it."

"So you felt empowered – did any other C feel empowered?" There were a few who said words like "yes", "sort of" and "at times".

There were also plenty of Cs who felt the opposite. "Thanks for your honesty. Let's talk about this later on. We are uncovering plenty of areas for further exploration. There are two more Cs we haven't heard from yet, so let's hear from them before we talk with the Bs."

The next C said, "It was all confusing. I felt uncertain about what I should be doing, there seemed to be a few people who knew what they had to do, but for me it was a waste of time."

"I hear what you are saying," I commented, "when we have finished our review maybe we can come back to your point. Perhaps you may change your mind, we'll see."

The final C took over: "It wasn't so much of a waste of time for me but I didn't get involved that much. There was no system in place to help us communicate effectively, and after trying to suggest this to my B, I sort of gave up. Maybe that's my fault and I should have persevered. I don't know."

It was time to wrap up the feelings from the Cs and move on to the Bs. I summarised: "Thank you Cs for your honesty about how you felt during that session. You have provided the group with plenty of food for thought and we will return to all these points in due course."

Remember, Brian Jeffers and his exec team were a part of this C population. I'll let you make your own minds up as to which of the C comments were from each of them. I needed to move on. "We are now going to find out how the Bs and the A felt, so let's start with the three Bs."

B-LEVEL FEELINGS

"Let us start with B1. Remember, this is not about the person, it is purely about the role, but I would like to hear how you felt during the game, please," I said, getting ready to add some words to the B flip chart.

"Totally puzzled by what was happening. The Cs clearly knew what they were doing and I became the conduit between them and the A. I seemed to be ignored by A and never got a reply to my questions. I tried to help and when the Cs passed me a pile of cards for A, I quickly passed them on. I then got a request from A for all the cards to be passed to him, so I asked my Cs and also the other two Bs."

"But how did that make you feel?"

"I did enjoy myself, and when I got the request from A I finally felt useful. I could do something constructive but I didn't get much support from the other Bs."

This was interesting and I planned to explore it further, but first of all I wanted to hear from the others. "Thank you, we'll come back to your point. How about B2? How did you feel?"

"I found that tough, a bit like the other B. It was confusing and I just felt like I was a postbox for the A and Cs to communicate with each other."

"That's right," interrupted B3, "I was squeezed in all directions; the Cs kept giving me notes and if I didn't reply quickly, I got another one asking the same question."

"Me too – it got to the point that I couldn't think about prioritising what I received, I just tried to clear as much as I could to make me feel better."

This was added to the flip chart and I asked, "Anything else before we move on to A?"

B3 replied: "I started getting requests for things but had no idea why I was being asked for them; it made me quite angry, actually. I felt as though some people had their own agenda and didn't want to share it with others." She continued: "It was only in the last few minutes I started to feel good as my Cs came up with the solution and I passed it up to the A. I'm pleased we got there in the end, albeit in a frustrating way."

This prompted a response from B1: "When I passed you a message asking for the cards, you just sent me a quick one-word reply back saying 'WHY?' That seemed aggressive to me and I couldn't understand why you were being like it."

Time for me to step in. "These are all valid points and nothing I haven't seen or heard before after groups have played this game. I promise we will come back to them all at some stage. If it's okay with you, let's move on to the A for a few minutes."

A-LEVEL FEELINGS

"You've waited patiently listening to the Bs and Cs. How are you feeling right now?"

"I can't believe what I'm hearing. I'm really disappointed with myself for what happened…"

I interrupted A "Let's be very clear here, this is not about you; it is just about this role in the game and, I guess, to a certain extent this role in an organisation or team. Please don't take it to heart, it's not about you – is that clear?"

"Okay," he said, "but I just can't believe what I'm hearing. It seemed to me that everyone was busy trying to resolve the task, but all I'm now hearing is that no one even knew what the task was. It can only be because the Bs didn't pass the message on."

"Let's not look for where things went wrong right now or who is to blame. I'm still tying to establish how different roles felt during the activity. Tell me, how did you actually feel during the game?"

"I felt quite uncomfortable most of the time. I couldn't see what was going on behind me. I could hear that there was plenty of activity; people seemed to be enjoying themselves as there was loads of sniggering and laughter, but I wasn't in control of what was going on. I got frustrated on several occasions when I sent the task to a B and, although I thought that he understood what was needed, I wasn't sure that the others knew."

"That's interesting," I said adding a few more words to the flip chart. "So let's be clear; there was a task to achieve in the 25 minutes, was there?"

"Yes, and I sent it to the Bs on several occasions – that's why I can't understand what I'm hearing."

"What? What was the task then?" asked several Cs at the same time.

Before A could respond, I quickly interjected: "All will be revealed shortly, although I can guarantee that there was a task set. A, are there any other feelings you had that may help us understand what you were experiencing?"

"Well, everyone seemed to be looking to me for the answers. I sensed some responsibility to give them the answers they were looking for, and because of that it felt like the pressure was on me to come up with a solution. Finally, towards the end when a B finally gave me the answer to the task, I felt relieved – it was as if they had listened to me after all and gone about working it out. I was quite confident then that we had cracked it. I'm not so sure now, though!"

"Thanks A. That seems like a whole mixture of emotions in just a short space of time – you must be exhausted. Thanks again for taking on the A role. It's not an easy one and I needed someone in that role with broad shoulders, and you haven't let me down."

I went back to the flip charts and said: "I want to just summarise all these feelings I've captured on the flip chart. With 18 Cs, clearly there is a longer list, so let's start with them."

SUMMARY

'C' Feelings

- Left out
- Confused
- Not included
- Ignored
- Disinterested
- Great
- Needed
- In the dark
- Happy
- Not pressurised
- Guilty
- Bored

- Couldn't be bothered
- Isolated
- Frustrated
- Relaxed
- Concerned
- Not needed
- Useless
- Not trusted
- Out of control
- Empowered
- Wasted time
- Uncertainty

'B' Feelings

- Puzzled
- The conduit
- Ignored
- Useful
- Piggy in the middle
- A post box

- Squeezed
- No time, unplanned
- Angry
- Pleased
- Frustrated

'A' Feelings

- Disappointed
- Blind
- Satisfied
- Uncomfortable

- Pressurised
- Relieved

"I suggest you take some time to reflect on these words, maybe consider whether this is how you, or your people, are feeling back at work. We'll pick up more of what the causes of these feelings are as we go through the next phase in the review, but for now has anyone any observations or questions?"

"It strikes me," suggested A, "that the negative feeling isn't just at the C level; it runs across all the levels. It looks to me as though this is all driven by a lack of feeling useful."

I noticed a few puzzled faces around the room. "Explain to me a bit more about what you mean by that," I said.

"I mean we didn't seem to have any purpose to our roles; we had nothing significant to do and ultimately felt undervalued."

"That's a very good observation," I replied. "It's what we call meaningfulness, which is driven by emotion and therefore it's about needing to feel the job is worthwhile, that there is a point to it, and that we are being useful in achieving what is required. Research has recently shown that having a real sense of belonging increases our meaningfulness and in the case of playing this game, I suspect there wasn't much feeling of belonging and of all being in it together. I liked the way you explained it as feeling significant and valued."

"So what you are saying is that we would have been happier in what we were doing if we had felt useful?" asked a B.

"Let me explain a bit further," I said. "There is a direct correlation between happiness and meaningfulness, and you could say they are inextricably linked, but in reality they don't always fit together. For example, you can feel happy if you are getting everything you want, but you may not feel valued in what you do. In other words, one could say that feeling happy is about taking, and meaningfulness is much more about giving. I firmly believe that people who attain meaning from what they do are much more engaged and likely to stay in that organisation, become more productive and be a key player in its success."

I needed to move on, so I said: "It's an interesting discussion and perhaps something we should explore further at a later date; but for now I would like to get back to reviewing, if that's okay with you?"

"We need purpose in our lives, to feel significant and valued. Perhaps meaningfulness is about giving and therefore providing a purpose."

THE BEGINNING OF THE END

It was time to continue with the review and start to share across the group how they all behaved.

"We are going to spend some time looking at what actually happened during the game and try to understand perhaps why things didn't work out the way they were intended. Before we get to review your understanding of what the task was, and what you think the answer to the task was, I thought you might like to hear some of the messages that were being exchanged. With a large group often one side of the room has no idea what the other side of the room is doing, so let me read a few of the messages out from the ones I collected as the game progressed. I've tried to keep them in rough chronological order."

I picked up the notes I had collected during the game and prepared to read them out. "So the first message was written only 15 seconds after I announced the start and you could begin writing notes. This was closely followed by a flurry of activity and messages changing hands in all directions. I think we need to come back to that point a bit later."

And so I started to read the messages out. "The first one I picked up simply said 'I'm confused'. This was from one C to another C. Totally expected, let's face it – you had been given the rules on playing a 'game', but actually no game."

"'What is the task?' was the next message and a common one from Cs to Cs, Cs to Bs, Bs to the A and to the Cs. Surprisingly, there was also the same message from A to a B.'

"'What are you doing?' was sent from one C to another C."

"'I don't know,' came the reply from the C!"

There was a roar of laughter from everyone.

"This next collection was a short conversation between two Cs:

'I haven't got any cards.'

'Why not?'

'He didn't give me any.' (referring to me)

'Ask for some.'

'Can I have a look at yours?'

'I don't know if I'm allowed to show you them.'

'It can't do any harm.'

'Here you are.' She handed over her full pack of cards.

'Thanks.'

'Keep half of them and pass the rest back.'

'Okay, let's see if we get told off for that.'

"B to A," I said.

"'What do you want us to do?'

'Make some tea please.'" More laughter.

"And then a few messages from Cs to Bs around seven minutes into the game:

'Can I go to the men's room please?'

'Is A okay?'

'Do the other Bs know what the task is?'

'Can I have a pay rise please?'

'Shall we collect the cards into packs of the same picture?'

'We all have cards with pictures, any idea what to do with them?'

'I'm bored!'

'You look busy, need any help?'

'I have a musical note here, should we make up a song?'

'The red cow flies south tonight.'

'Thanks for the kick up the backside, much needed!'

"And of course, some of the responses from the Bs to the Cs:

'NO!'

'I think he's gone to sleep, best we leave him alone.'
'I asked but negative.'
'Grow up.'
'Why not, it gives you something to do. Report back when done.'
'Collect them into packs of similar picture. Tell the others.'
'Find something to do.'
'I'm fine thanks.'
'That sounds like fun.'
'What???'
'My pleasure. Now look busy.'"

I continued, "Whilst the Bs were responding to the Cs they also had to field some messages and requests from A. Here's a sample of a few of the early A messages. We'll hear some later ones shortly.

'What are you doing?'
'Have you got the task?'
'Nope.'
'You sound busy, can I do anything to help?'
'What are the Cs doing?'
'Please find out what symbols the Cs have.'
'What have you found out for me?'
'I need you to find out the common symbols.'
'Tell the Cs to hurry up.'
'Have you got the answer yet?'"

At this point several of the Cs let out gasps of surprise. "What, you had a task all the time and told the Bs what it was?" came a challenge from one of them.

Closely followed by more Cs questions about why they didn't know the task.

"I never got the task sent to me," retorted B1.

This naturally prompted B2 to become defensive and pass the blame back to A for not sending the task to the Bs. "Me neither, I wish I had received it but A didn't pass it on," and looking directly at A, said, "I can't believe you had it all the time and didn't tell us what we were meant to be doing. No wonder it was a shambles."

"But I did send it to you – in fact, several times. You clearly didn't read it!" reacted A.

"Hold on," I said, "these are fair challenges but for now let's finish this part of the review so that we all have an understanding of some of the frustrations you encountered during the game. Is that okay?" I asked.

After a few nods and mutters of acceptance, we were ready to resume. "So let's continue with a few of the messages the Bs were sending to the A; after all, they did manage to communicate with A at times." I started to read out some more messages collected during the game.

"'What do you want us to do?'
'We need some direction here.'
'Have you got a task?'
'Do you want sugar in your tea?'"

Laughter ensued and the group started to relax again, so I carried on with a few more messages.

"'The Cs want to know what to do.'
'Would you like to see the cards?'
'Can I have a pay rise?'
'The Cs have a plan.'
'They think it's the musical note.'"

"On and on these messages went, back and forth between all three levels in the game. So let's get down to understanding what the task was. Wait though, before I ask A to confirm what he was set to achieve let us have a look at all of your understanding of what the task was," I said, as I went to the Post-it® notes positioned on the flip chart.

I started to read some of the notes. "It's quite evident that the C population didn't have any idea what the task was; in fact, I can see that over half either put a question mark, or said no idea! A couple thought it was to group like symbols, some thought it was to find the odd one out, one C decided it was to pass all the cards to A. Oh dear, and one here believed it was to find out everyone's favourite music!"

"What!" exclaimed A, "that's just plain idiotic – it's all made up."

"We'll understand why this happened soon enough," I said, and then moved to the B's notes. "Okay, the first B thought the task was to identify the odd one out, which links in to what some of the Cs thought; the next B understood it as to be able to demonstrate effective communication and the final B thought it was to find the common symbols; three different views, which probably explains why the Cs didn't have much of an idea about what the task was."

"So it is the Bs' fault, then," interjected a C. "Remember," I needed to keep making this point,

"it's not about apportioning blame or who to attribute success or failure to; it's about understanding the causes of the problem. We are only in step 2 of resolving your organisational problem. Let me explain this a bit further."

I went to a clean flip chart and wrote the first step:

1. Recognise the very existence of the problem

"This sounds basic, but if you think about it, some problems are big and 'in-your-face', mostly technical problems that can be identified easily but not necessarily easily rectified. However, there are times when things are just not working. Technically everything is in order and working well, but productivity is not as it should be; in this instance it could be easy to believe that there is no problem at all. On balance, things are working as they should do. Putting your finger on the problem could prove difficult," I said.

"For your organisation, it's evident that you have already achieved step 1; after all, we are here today because Brian and the exec team have recognised that there is some issue that needs resolving, but at this point in time are struggling to identify what it is. Today we have moved to step 2."

I added to the flip chart the second step:

1. **Recognise the very existence of the problem**
2. **Understand the problem**

"So we are trying to understand what the problem is. Why does it occur? However, identifying the problem doesn't explain what's causing it. Finding the cause will help suggest solutions. Let me explain a bit further. If every time you look at the clock it shows the time as 11.25, after several glances over a few minutes we will recognise there is a problem with the clock (that's step 1 completed). Now, as we have discovered, there is a problem with the clock working, but at this point we don't know what's causing it not to work. So what could be the causes?"

"The battery is dead," offered B1.

"So do we just go and change the battery?" I asked. "Well, it could actually be broken," suggested a C.

"In that case, it would be pointless changing the battery," I replied.

"It might be an electric clock and just not plugged into a socket," suggested someone else.

"Now we have a different problem, then. What may be the cause of an electric clock not working?"

"It's not plugged in, or perhaps it might have blown a fuse, or maybe there could be a power cut," came a reply.

And another suggestion: "It may have a faulty connection somewhere."

"Aha, so there are many things that could be causing the problem to exist," I said. "We cannot just charge in trying to solve the problem of the clock not working if we have no idea what the cause is. It's the same for your business. Today is about trying to identify what is causing your organisational problem right now. Playing this game will hopefully help to achieve this.

"Although we won't be moving on to the other steps today, it's important that you know what they are. It will help you over the coming days, weeks and months. Let's go through them," and I wrote the third step on the flip chart.

1. ***Recognise the very existence of the problem***
2. ***Understand the problem***
3. ***Know your organisation well enough***

"It may seem a ridiculous step," I explained, "but I have come across many leadership teams that just don't know their organisation well enough to be able to identify where the problem exists and therefore where to concentrate our efforts. You see, without knowing where it exists, we will still be at an impasse. Through my conversations with Brian, I am fairly certain that's not the case here."

Now I added step 4.

1. ***Recognise the very existence of the problem***
2. ***Understand the problem***

3. *Know your organisation well enough*
4. *Establish what the situation should be like*

"Let's face it, we need some direction here; we need to establish what it would be like if the problem didn't exist. There's no point in setting out on a journey if you have no idea where you want to get to. In the days of maps, when satellite navigation didn't exist, when we were about to drive to a new destination, the first thing we did was to look for where we wanted to get to, then we looked for our current location and planned our route accordingly. I call this the 'Change Loop'. Therefore, in this step, we need to look at what our desired state should be like," I said. "Without it we have no direction and that can be a disaster for any organisation," I added. "This leads us nicely into the next step in the process," I said, adding step 5 to the flip chart.

1. *Recognise the very existence of the problem*
2. *Understand the problem*
3. *Know your organisation well enough*
4. *Establish what the situation should be like*
5. *Establish the shortfalls*

"Now we know where we want to get to, we have to work out how to get there. Basically, it's what we need to do to move from where we are to where we want to be. In effect, we need to establish our shortfalls. At this point we need to evaluate employee, department and organisational progress versus our company goals. There is a need for the leadership team to compare actual performance against step 4. This will enable us to determine what issues need to be addressed, and help to create a plan to ensure its achievement." I added step 6 to the flip chart.

1. *Recognise the very existence of the problem*
2. *Understand the problem*

3. Know your organisation well enough
   4. Establish what the situation should be like
   5. Establish the shortfalls
   6. Develop a leadership plan to achieve step 4

"Step 6 is not necessarily the final step. I'll explain what I mean in a minute. The reality is that even the best solution is destined not to succeed if a plan for its implementation isn't developed. It has to clearly identify how we are going to get from where we currently are to where we want to be. Now, it's all very well having a robust plan, but it is worthless unless we add in steps 7, 8 and 9. Whilst these first six steps are the basics for solving an organisational problem, in itself it's not enough – at some point we have to implement the solution, so here we have step 7."

   1. Recognise the very existence of the problem
   2. Understand the problem
   3. Know your organisation well enough
   4. Establish what the situation should be like
   5. Establish the shortfalls
   6. Develop a leadership plan to achieve step 4
   7. Implement the plan

"This step is about committing fully to your plan and putting it into action. Experience tells me that by far the most effective approach is to involve as many other people in the implementation phase to ensure there is minimal resistance to any changes that may occur," I said. "Think about the game – how many of you felt involved? Probably not many and, consequently, there was little feeling of meaningfulness. Remember the discussion we had about feeling significant and valued? Involving people – the Cs will build this feeling.

"And so to the final step," and I added step 8 to the flip chart.
1. **Recognise the very existence of the problem**
2. **Understand the problem**
3. **Know your organisation well enough**
4. **Establish what the situation should be like**
5. **Establish the shortfalls**
6. **Develop a leadership plan to achieve step 4**
7. **Implement the plan**
8. **Monitor and evaluate progress**

'I may challenge my last comment in a minute, but let's look at this step first. It's all very well implementing the solution, but we need to know how successful it is or has been; so during our planning stage we must build in some feedback channels to create ongoing monitoring and testing of reality against our expectations. If there is little to no improvement, then an alternative solution could be sought and ultimately implemented.

"Okay," I continued, "I said I may challenge my previous comment so let me ask you a question. Is step 8, 'monitor and evaluate progress', the final step in the process?"

"I'm not sure there's much left to do except go through the process again," offered a B.

"Thanks for that," I said, "has anyone got another view?" "Perhaps as an exec team we could celebrate a successful implementation?" suggested Mary, the HR Director.

"Excellent. If we could add one more step to this process, I would add in one about recognising our success, communicating it to all levels in the organisation and celebrating it." And I added the step to the flip chart.
1. **Recognise the very existence of the problem**
2. **Understand the problem**
3. **Know your organisation well enough**

4. **Establish what the situation should be like**
5. **Establish the shortfalls**
6. **Develop a leadership plan to achieve step 4**
7. **Implement the plan**
8. **Monitor and evaluate progress**
9. **Recognise, communicate and celebrate success**

"This step is repeatedly forgotten in organisations. Only too frequently do leaders fail to recognise individual and team contributions to organisational success. At the heart of this, communication is fundamental to continued success. People have a real desire for information about how we/they are doing. They have a need to know what their contribution is delivering to the overall goal. Delivering step 9 will develop an air of confidence, a desire to go further and, ultimately, a culture of continuous improvement."

I finished off by offering one final challenge to the group. "Consider this – and I'm not looking for anyone to answer the question right now – but how often over the last year has anyone received any recognition for a job well done? Or think about this: as you are all leaders, how many of you have recognised others' contributions? One has to be honest with oneself to understand the true answer; indeed, some food for thought."

"I hope this has helped you understand where we are today and what lies ahead of us. Now let's get back to the review."

'So what was the task?' asked B2.

"That's a good question," I replied, "but before we ask A to explain what it was, I think we should just have a look at what you believed the answer was," and I returned to the flip chart with the Post-it® Notes.

"Evidently, if there was no understanding of what the task was, it would be impossible to establish what the answer was. You may have got lucky with a guess, but obviously, in business, guessing is detrimental to organisational success. There is an array of answers as I would have expected from the Cs; some of you wrote 'No idea,' others have just drawn a question mark. There's a couple who thought the answer was the musical note and a small group decided the answer was the winner's cup. The most interesting answer here is the number 42," – laughter erupted again. "Clearly a lover of *The Hitchhiker's Guide to the Galaxy*!" I added. "And as for the three Bs, like some of the Cs, one B thought it was the winner's cup and the other two were undecided: they didn't know. A fair reflection of their understanding of what the task was, I think."

I wanted to move on and pick up on the key messages from the game, so it was time to reveal the actual task and appreciate why things went so wrong. I turned back to the flip chart.

"Now A had a task to achieve, and this is what he has written on his Post-it® Note as the task: 'to determine the common symbols the Cs have'. Is that the task?" I asked A. "Yes it is," came the reply; he then added, "and I sent that message to the Bs, so I cannot understand why they now say they didn't know what it was."

"That's a fair argument. However, let's be very clear about the task, and this is an important point. Can you read the task out word for word from the card I gave you at the start of the game, please."

A retrieved the card from the pack he had accumulated and read: "Your task is to determine which symbol the Cs have in common."

"Right, here's the first problem we had. The task is quite clear – it was to determine which symbol the Cs had in common. The interpretation was in the plural, as was written on the Post-it® 'to determine the common symbols the Cs have'. It's a basic error, but one that is all too often repeated. Why might that be?" I asked.

"It wasn't easy having to write everything on Post-it® Notes. I was trying to get the message out to the Bs quickly," came the reply.

In support, one of the Bs added, "I agree, I was trying to shorten answers as much as possible. I couldn't write fast enough to keep up with all the messages I was receiving."

"But if it was written on a card, why didn't you just copy what the card said?" suggested a C.

I interjected: "Here is our first difficulty. We all interpret what we read in our own model of the world, and we will emphasise key words that fit within our own thought patterns. This can be a catalyst for disaster, and the further a message is passed through an organisation, the more it will be interpreted by others and possibly end up becoming totally distorted. This could be attributed to our desire to short-circuit or simplify what we do."

"So what you're saying is that we naturally interpret what we read and make it fit our own model of the world?"

"Of course," I replied, "we have to decode any message we receive, in whatever format it is sent and it can get us into trouble, as we have experienced here."

"I still don't understand why the task never filtered through to the Cs, though," said the A.

"Let's explore that point then. How many Bs did you send the task to?" I asked.

"At lease two of them," he said.

"Correct. I picked up your messages to B1 and B2, but nothing was sent to B3. In fact, you sent the task, written differently both times, to B1 on two occasions."

"I didn't receive the task from A, though," said B2.

The Cs were starting to look bemused by what they were hearing. "The task was sent to you but you didn't receive it? How can that be?"

I offered a solution. "It's quite simple, really. When the messages were given to B2, they immediately went to the bottom of the pile of messages accumulating whilst B2 continued to reply to the onslaught of messages from you Cs. It's safe to say at this point in time that everyone played a part in the demise of the task. I would like to explore each of the levels again, and inparticular I'm interested to hear what each level could have done differently."

"Every meaning is a direct derivative of interpretation."

RETROSPECTION IS A WONDERFUL THING

"This time let's start with the A. I must stress that this is not the time for a character assassination, but an opportunity to understand a bit more about the role of A and the responsibilities they have. So tell me, what could A have done differently?"

WHAT A COULD HAVE DONE DIFFERENTLY

"I should have been clearer about the task," started A. "I realise now that I got it wrong. If I had made certain that all the Bs knew exactly what it was we had to achieve, we may well have accomplished it."

"Okay, so the first thing perhaps this level needs to consider is how to set a clear direction for its people. That's on the assumption they have a direction, of course! What could A have done, then?" I asked.

"Made sure the Cs understood the task." "Offered ideas on how to achieve it."

"Maybe confirmed that the Bs understood the task!" "He could have told the Bs to get the Cs to tell them what information they all had," suggested A. "How would that have helped?" I challenged.

"Well, the Bs could then have worked out how to complete the task and determined the common symbol – or at least get me involved," he replied.

"Let's explore this a bit further then," I said. "I believe there's another key message here. Perhaps the next thing A needs to do is to clarify all the Bs' understanding of the task, and to make sure they are all on the same page."

I continued, "The next thing A does is critical. It should be the simplest thing in the world to do, but is often the most difficult. Has anyone any idea what A should do, now that the Bs have a clear understanding of what the task is?" I quizzed.

"Support the Bs and let them know he is there if needed," suggested someone.

"Nothing!" said a C.

"Excellent, I'm with you there," I came back. "Once A has established that the Bs have a common understanding of the task, it's time to leave them alone to mobilise the staff to complete it. It's called empowerment! After all, Theodore Roosevelt, the US President was absolutely right when he said:

'The best executive is one who has sense enough to pick good people to do what he wants done, and self-restraint enough to keep from meddling with them while they do it.'

"What A should do after clarifying that all the Bs have a clear understanding of the task is to leave them alone to get on with completing it," I said. "This is the point where the A can go and play golf! Or better still, work on some of the more strategic issues the organisation may have. The problem here is that the A will often meddle in the completion of the task, from trying to direct the Bs in how he or she wants it completed to – at the extreme – trying to complete the task themselves. And trust me, on many occasions I have seen this happen. Roosevelt got it right. If you have recruited the right people to do a job for you, then trust them to do what you want done. So there are some messages from the A to the Bs we should have a look at," and I reread a handful of messages:

"'What are you doing?'
'What are the Cs doing?'
'What have you found out for me?' 'Tell the Cs to hurry up'
'Have you got the answer yet?'

"These messages are, in the main, not constructive; they don't help the process or aid achievement and, in many cases, get in the way of progress, slowing down the possibility of a successful outcome. Why is it that some leaders find it difficult to let go and trust their people to do the job?" I asked.

"It's as you say – they don't trust their people to do the job," offered a C.

"Perhaps they don't want to feel as though they have lost control. Being involved means they know what's going on all the time," suggested another. "Sometimes there is only one person who can do the job. No one will be able to do it better than the leader, and after all, they are the leader because they have the technical expertise." "Well, there's a really interesting point," I interrupted. "Technical expertise versus leadership capability. It's a challenge that we must explore, but one that will have to wait for another day, I'm afraid. Why else would a leader not trust or empower their people?"

One of the exec team offered: "Perhaps there just isn't time to empower others to do the job; it takes time to explain and train what needs to be done, and it's just simpler to get on and do it yourself."

"A very good point you make. However, what happens next time you have a task to be completed?" I asked.

A chorus of responses erupted. "You just do it yourself all over again and are now wasting time."

"Precisely," I agreed.

"If I'm being honest," someone added, "I actually don't like to give away some of the jobs that I like doing. In fact, I probably do a lot of jobs that other people could do, but I get pleasure from doing them myself."

Then came some support from others. "I guess that's the same for all of us – we do what we like doing."

"How idiotic is that? But we do."

"This is a definite problem some people have with delegating and empowering others," I agreed.

"Why would you want to do jobs just because you like doing them?" challenged a C.

"It makes me enjoy my work more," came a reply. "Okay, we have a potential conflict of views here," I said. "On the one hand we may not delegate some tasks because we like doing them and it may make our job more enjoyable – so if we love doing it, why not keep it? But on the other hand, it may come across as being self-centred, hanging on to what you like doing, rather than allowing the opportunity for the team to develop further by giving them the chance to take on the task. Maybe we'll come up with a definitive answer later. We are getting a whole array of reasons why leaders find it difficult to let go. Let's just recap what we've come up with." I went to the flip chart and started the list:

There is no trust
Don't want to lose control
No one can do it better
Not enough time
I do what I like doing

"This is a good start. There are a few other reasons I can think of, so let's add these to the list," I said. "Perhaps sometimes the leader feels that if they do not complete the task, then others will get the credit for it. It's a shame, as leaders need to be able to share the credit to ensure that their team becomes better than them. A bold statement and, again, something to be explored on another day." I added this to the list:

There is no trust
Don't want to lose control
No one can do it better
Not enough time
I do what I like doing
Others will be credited for it

"And to add a couple of other points, sometimes it may be that the leader just doesn't have the confidence in a team member to complete the task. Clearly, one has to explore why this may be. Is it down to lack of technical capability at this point in time, or is it more far-reaching than that?"

There is no trust
Don't want to lose control
No one can do it better
Not enough time
I do what I like doing
Others will be credited for it
Little or no confidence in a team member

"The final reason I would like to share with you – and in a way this links in to all of the others, in that the leader may feel that if they empower their people, they are empowering themselves out of a job. My challenge here is surely that's what they should be trying to do as a leader." I wrote this point on the flip chart also.

There is no trust
Don't want to lose control
No one can do it better

Not enough time
I do what I like doing
Others will be credited for it
Little or no confidence in a team member
Empowered out of a job

"That's all very well," added A, "but have you ever come across people who sometimes actually don't want to be empowered?"

"A very good question and the simple answer is yes. It's a fact that some of your people may have trouble accepting the notion of being empowered and – just like the leaders – there are many reasons why."

"As a C, I can think of several reasons," one of them answered. "A bit like the leader, I may not have enough time to take on additional responsibility; it is sometimes easier for the leader just to tell me what to do, and then I go off and do it. That's assuming I have the right skill level to be able to do it, of course."

Another C added, "Maybe we are more worried about getting it wrong. At the end of the day, if it goes wrong we are going to be blamed for it, so maybe it's best to do what we are told, rather than take it upon ourselves to make decisions."

I went back to the flip chart and turned over to a new sheet. "Let's capture these points; they are really valuable," I said, and started to add them to the new sheet.

Not enough time
Having the right skill level
Fear of getting it wrong/failure

"I'm not sure we have a blame culture here, though," defended one of the exec team. "I don't agree with that last point."

"We are only discussing this in general terms. It's for you to decide your culture and how you behave within it," I said. "What other reasons could there be for not wanting empowerment?"

"Well, perhaps the person just doesn't think it's their job."

"And if I take this on, maybe I am being used to take the fall if something goes wrong," suggested someone else.

"Thanks for that; a couple of other barriers there. Let's add these to our list and then get back to our review," I said.

Not enough time
Having the right skill level
Fear of getting it wrong/failure
Being used to take the fall
It's not my job

"This comes all the way back to recognising that trust is an important part within teams and an organisation. Without it, progress will be hindered to the point that success is unlikely."

Eager to move on, I said, "There's certainly some big messages here and I hope you are getting something from it. I'd like to get back to the review once again. We've established that, first, A needs to set a clear direction. Once this is done, he or she needs to ensure that there is a common understanding, and then go and play golf! What else could A have done in this task to help it succeed?"

"Why didn't A turn around and see what was happening?" came the first suggestion.

"I wasn't allowed to," said A quickly, "I was told to sit like this facing the wall."

"Who said you had to sit that way?" I challenged.

"You did," he retorted, "when you gave out the instructions at the beginning."

"Interesting, because I deliberately didn't say that; I wanted to challenge a paradigm that this role often has. It seems to me that there is an assumption that you cannot challenge rules. Let me put it this way: I positioned the chair to face away from everyone else for a specific reason."

"But why would you do that? It just made things more difficult," replied the A.

"I'm trying to replicate reality," I replied. "In many organisations, including yours, the CEO, A in this case, may not be based in the same country, let alone the same building. By facing the A away from everyone else, it suggests they are not in the same room. The A is aware there is a lot of activity going on in his or her organisation or function, but often will not be close enough to understand exactly what that activity is. Again, it is about trusting your people to do the job they are employed to do. However, there is a caveat to that, of course, and this goes all the way back to the A setting a clear direction and ensuring that there is a common understanding of that direction," I reminded them. "So in this game, what could A have done?"

"If he had turned his chair around, or even got up and looked, he may have had a better understanding of what was going on," came the suggestion.

"I agree with you. Challenge that paradigm and take a risk occasionally. There was no risk in the game, but there will be in the workplace. However, it's about taking the right risks for the right reasons," I said. "There is another important lesson here that was made popular in the 1980s, and most of you will know it as MBWA, (Management By Walking About). It's the idea that, as a manager/leader, we need to get in the habit of stopping and talking with people face-to-face, to get an idea of how they believe things are going, and to listen to whatever they have on their minds. During the game, A was aware that there was a lot going on behind him, there was plenty of activity; but in reality, he had no idea what the activity was. Maybe by walking about the A may have picked up on something that was amiss. I hope that makes sense," I added.

"It's time to leave the A role alone for a while and maybe we should now concentrate on the Bs. So let's ask the same question: what could the Bs have done differently during the game?"

WHAT THE BS COULD HAVE DONE DIFFERENTLY

"Well, they could have clarified the task with A," suggested the first C.

That caused a response from one of the Bs. "I thought we did, though. I kept asking A what the task was —what he wanted us to do – but I didn't seem to get a reply."

"As you now know, I did send the task to the Bs on several occasions. Okay, I admit, it was not word-perfect, but even my interpretation of the task didn't filter down to the Cs," he replied.

"I just couldn't cope with all the messages," said another B. "I just simply missed the important requests in amongst everything else that was going on, so maybe I should have worked out a way of prioritising what I had to do; after all, I just replied to whatever was on the top of my pile of messages. Maybe that's the biggest message for me," she added.

"As they were so busy with messages, why couldn't the Bs have sent a message to all the Cs asking them to stop sending messages until they were clear on what the task was?" came another suggestion.

"Again, some great points. First, I agree; the Bs' responsibility here is to understand the task and confirm with A that understanding. They also have a responsibility to ensure that all of their level is on the same page; that they have a common understanding of the task," I said. "Of course, this would mean communicating amongst themselves. Here's a question for the Bs: how many times did you communicate with each other?" I asked.

"Not enough," one said.

"Not at all!" another replied.

"A couple of times with the B next to me, but that's about it really," said the third B.

"Hardly a recipe for successfully achieving a common goal, is it?" I said, making the point clear. I went on, "As for the suggestion of asking the Cs to stop what they were doing and just wait, how successful do you think that would have been?" I asked.

"It could have been almost impossible to stop us Cs. We were busy enjoying ourselves, making tasks up and generally misbehaving!"

I pondered this response. "You make a valid point there. It is very easy to create chaos and often very difficult to create order from chaos. In this situation, it would be hard to suppress the energy at the C level; however, all the messages the Bs were receiving was noise getting in the way, and something has to be done," I said. "Let's look at something else. Assuming the Bs had agreed a common goal amongst themselves and with the A, what could the Bs do next?"

"Tell us Cs what it is – it's that simple," came the reply.

"Absolutely, it's not rocket science here; at some stage the Cs need to know what the task is, and what the Bs' expectations of them are."

"That's a fair point," one of the Bs said, "we didn't give them a chance, did we?"

"No, you didn't. Now let me ask another question, and you have one vote each here: which level do you think was best placed to achieve the task today? Who votes for A?"

Four hands went up. "For the Bs?"

Six votes.

"So that would make 12 people believing the Cs were in the best position to achieve the task. Those who think the A is best placed, why do you say that?" I asked.

"Quite simply, he has the task, he knows what needs to be done," came the reply.

"Okay, thanks for that. What about those of you who voted for the Bs?"

"They are in the middle of it. They could get the task from A and they could then collect the information from the Cs and work it out between them." "And there are fewer of them, so they could work together more easily," offered another person.

"Okay, and what about those who thought the Cs were in the best position to achieve the task?"

"Providing we were given the correct task and early on," said a C, "we must be the ones to complete it. We have all the cards, and there are more of us to do the work."

"I agree," said another, "it goes back to what you were saying about picking the right people and sense enough to let them get on and do the job."

I smiled. "Absolutely right. As leaders, we must always remember what Roosevelt said:

'The best executive is one who has sense enough to pick good people to do what he wants done, and self-restraint enough to keep from meddling with them while they do it.'

"In my view," I said, carrying on, "the Cs were the people best placed to achieve this task. As you said, they had all the cards. In this game, the cards are a metaphor for information – data, if you like – and the Cs had the information. So what should the Bs have done after telling the Cs what the task was?"

"I get it now; as Bs we should empower the Cs to get on and complete the task, and then go and play golf with the A." This brought much laughter.

"Who agrees?" I challenged. There were a handful of nods and yesses. "So some of you agree, but those of you who don't agree: what should the Bs do next?"

"Like the A should do with the Bs; they should clarify the Cs understanding of the task to ensure that they are all aligned and working towards the same goal, maybe?" proposed a B.

"And," added the A, "they should then be available to support the Cs should they need it!"

"Right." I was feeling pleased. "These are both great suggestions. So the Bs need to ensure there is consistency of message across their own people and across all the teams. What sort of support should the Bs offer?"

"If you had asked me that question yesterday, I would probably have said that the Bs would need to support them in developing the process to complete the task, but now I'm not so sure," came a response.

"That's the same for me," added the A, "perhaps once the Bs have set what needs to be done, it should be up to the Cs to determine how they are going to do it."

"There you go," I said, looking pleased, "you're starting to think slightly differently now. And yes, I totally agree, you set the 'What', but let your staff set the 'How'. As their leader, you should focus on the final result and not on the detail and how it's being done. The upshot is by empowering your people to determine how they will go about achieving the task, you can then use your time and expertise more wisely, where they will make a difference. Now back to the question: what support should the Bs offer the Cs?"

The group again pondered this question. "I think the Bs should be available to help if the Cs need them; so, for example, if they get stuck and can't see a way forward, maybe they could use the Bs as a sounding board," suggested a C.

The A added, "Yes, and maybe offer support through coaching, as opposed to just telling them the answers."

"That's a good idea," said a B, "it was made apparent to me on a management course I attended a few years ago that different people need different levels of support depending on their current capability; what I mean is, how skilled they are to do the job. Coaching would surely help develop their skill."

"What about the Bs supporting us by recognising the hard work we put in to achieving the task?"

"Yes, that doesn't happen often enough, as far as I'm concerned," came a comment from one of the Cs, with some nods of agreement from others.

I decided to summarise these suggestions. "Let's look at what you have suggested here. Once the Bs have a clear direction themselves, they need to set this direction with the Cs. That's not enough on its own; they then need to check that there is a common understanding, and that all the C population is aligned towards one unified aim. The Bs also need to ensure there is a clear understanding amongst the Cs of each individual's role and their responsibility.

"I agree with your next suggestion also; the Bs need to be available to support the Cs by whichever means is appropriate, recognising that their support will vary depending on not only individual's skill level, but also their desire, or will, to be involved and successfully achieve the task," I said.

"And picking up on your point about being recognised for your contribution," I went on, "in my experience virtually all organisations and their leaders/managers understand in theory that their people want, and need, to be recognised for a job well done. So the worry here is: why are they not very good at it? What people are really looking for is personal recognition from their manager. It doesn't have to be anything fancy; more often than not, it could be as simple as a pat on the back or the occasional word of praise, or a thank you. In reality, recognition costs nothing apart from a very small amount of time, but the rewards from doing it can be immeasurable."

I needed to add one final point to recognition. "There is a watch-out here, though. As one of the most quoted men of the 18th century, Samuel Johnson once said:

'He who praises everybody, praises nobody.'

"So beware; recognition can be overdone, resulting in it losing its meaning and impact."

"Well, that's food for thought," admitted A, "we need to do more of it but clearly not overdo it."

"Precisely what I was thinking," added a C.

I looked at Brian, who was smiling. "Great, let's leave it there for now. You have recognised another very clear message from playing the game. I want to move on to the C level now, and explore what the Cs were doing and perhaps investigate why. After all, you were extremely busy people, bearing in mind this was on the backdrop of not even having a task to complete. We'll then consider some of the things the Cs could perhaps have done differently." Looking around the group, I said, "So explain to me: why were you so busy?"

WHAT THE CS COULD HAVE DONE DIFFERENTLY

"Initially," offered the first C, "we seemed busy trying to find out what we were meant to be doing. I know a couple of Cs sat back and just waited, but most of us started asking for the task."

"I didn't have any cards to start with, so I was busy finding out why, and then if I should have some so I could contribute," said the C without any cards.

I needed to make a point here. "That's interesting," I said, "in all the times I have used the game – and it doesn't matter what industry or market it was in – 70 per cent of the time the C that didn't have any cards was the busiest person in the room. Why is that?"

There were a few seconds of laughter before the C explained, "Initially I was trying to find out why I didn't have any cards, and I still don't know," he said. "Then I wanted to see what the cards consisted of, in case I may have been able to offer some help in working out what the task was."

Another C added, "Isn't that a bit like in real life at work? Even if we don't have much work on, we always look busy; otherwise, we may be given additional work that may be less important and boring to do."

"Or worse still, be made redundant!" added another.

"It wasn't that at all. It was because I could help organise things, as I had less to do," defended the C. "It all changed when I was given some of the cards from the C next to me. I felt more involved and wanted to make use of them, so I carried on trying to get the Cs to work together."

I wanted to sum up this important point. "Well, if I was A here, and I visited your workplace, I would be really pleased with you. Let's face it, the Cs were really busy, there was plenty of laughter and they seemed to be enjoying their work. The Bs were communicating with the Cs and with me as the A, everything gave the impression of a really productive business. You would probably all have been given a pay rise, and yet the contribution to what I needed doing was just about zero."

After some murmurs of acknowledgement, I went on: "It's interesting that we feel as though we need to look busy at work, even if we haven't much to do. We feel the need to put on an act and deceive our bosses. I believe that putting on a show could well backfire eventually. Let me explain. It's no secret that people are fearful of being seen as not working hard and, ultimately, losing their jobs. The problem here is that managers become suspicious that their people are trying to be manipulative, and give a false impression of the amount of work they actually do that contributes to the company success. Let's be fair; managers more often than not will notice when busy people don't contribute to the bottom line. In reality, they recognise people who are busy not making money. Are those people just being busy fools?"

I carried on to make the point: "For you as managers, if your people always look busy, perhaps they're not really working at all. It's all a big show for you – they are probably trying to protect their job and impress you, their boss. Perhaps they should be allowed some down time to work on the things that are important, and not just work on the things that are urgent. We haven't got time today, but at some stage in the future we should take a look at this in more detail," I said.

"There is one more point I would like to make about the missing cards. Did anyone find them?" I asked, and received a resounding no.

"Well, you have had them all the time. I placed them on the empty chair right next to you two." And I pointed to the spare pack still on the chair.

"When did you put them there?" asked one of the Cs. "As I handed them out to everyone else," I answered. "The reason for doing this is to make the point that sometimes we have colleagues away on holiday or off sick; hence leaving an empty chair. Now, if we don't recognise that there are people not present to contribute to the task, it must be our responsibility to ensure that any information that the missing person/people has – in this case a pack of cards – is included in the work that is being done. Right now, though, let's explore a bit more about the C level and their behaviour," I said.

"They seemed to know what they were doing," said a B. "I thought they had the task because they were working in groups, and after a while were suggesting to us what the task was – and at one point, even giving us the solution."

"I thought that because we had all the cards, we could work out what needed to be done," said one C. "So we started to share ideas and finally agreed that, as I was the only person who had a picture of a cup with number 1 on it, the task must be to find the odd one out. How were we to know it was wrong?"

"You weren't," said A, "another group decided the task was to get all the cards to me, so they were clearly busy trying to achieve that; perhaps the Cs were busy trying to make a task up because of what we just talked about – they felt they needed to be busy."

Then a C said, "I saw the other side of the room were really busy, so I thought they must know what they were doing. It felt as though I was the only one who didn't know what was going on, so I asked them what they were doing."

"Did you find out?" asked A.

"Not really. They said they were trying to work out what to do and then asked me for all my cards. I asked why they wanted them, but they never told me."

"This is all natural human behaviour," I explained. "In its simplest form, most of us need to have something to achieve; a goal or a task. Without it we simply make one up for all the reasons we have mentioned before. The fact that there were at least three different interpretations of what need to be achieved was irrelevant. The Cs were busy, and that's what was important!"

"It's true, I couldn't think of anything worse than having nothing to do. It might be okay for a couple of days, but I would eventually go stir-crazy," said one of the Cs.

"Me too," added another. "It reminds me of the canoeist who faked his death in 2002. He was holed up in a small bedsit and eventually walked into a police station, claiming he had lost his memory. I guess that for him, time in prison was more appealing than spending any more time with nothing to do!"

I smiled. "It's a point well made. Once boredom kicks in – and this could be for many reasons; for example, the task might be seen as too easy, or maybe too hard; it could be because it's uninteresting – a 'C' will undoubtedly find a way to misbehave. Let us not forget that our people need something to do," I said. "What else did the Cs do?"

"They sent loads of messages to me," said a B. "Most of them were just nonsense, like 'Can I go home early today?' or 'Can I have a pay rise please?', or even 'The red cow flies south tonight!' – what's that all about? It just got in the way and bogged me down."

"They were playing a game," I replied. "They were doing what Cs do best; entertaining themselves by playing games."

"What?" exclaimed one of the exec team, "The C level will spend their day playing games and making things up? Surely not."

"Not all the time," I said, "but if they have no direction, no idea of what they are meant to be doing, they are likely to decide on their own direction, or just make themselves busy enjoying themselves. Either way, it is counterproductive to the organisational objectives. Think back to when you were at the C level; sometimes it's not a great place to be.

"There's something else we need to consider here, too," I said. "I call it intelligent misbehaviour. Let me explain. There are some people who will think they have more skills and work experience than the job actually requires and, indeed, they may be over-qualified for the job they are currently doing. These people will tend to engage in counterproductive work behaviours (CWB) more than the people who feel that the job requirements fit their level of capability. This misbehaviour could well be driven by the person feeling that what they are being employed to do is menial, and they develop a cynical view of the meaningfulness of their role and are wasting their time and skills coming to work."

"That's so true," agreed a C, "the main reason I am here in this job is because I left my previous company because I felt that the job I was doing was worthless. I wasn't being stretched in any way. I was starting to become disillusioned and didn't look forward to going to work. Fortunately, this job came along. I dread to think what I would be like now if I was still at the old company."

I added a point here. "This goes back to something we were talking about earlier – feeling useful and having a sense of meaningfulness."

A few nods of acknowledgement illustrated to me that there were more Cs in the room who had had similar experiences. "Thanks for being honest with us. I'm sure you will be stretched here and given the opportunity to utilise your full set of skills," I said.

"So we recognise some of the C-level behaviour during the game; let's think about what the Cs could have done differently, then."

"Well, in retrospect, if I was to play the game again," offered a C, "I would wait for the Bs to give me some specific instructions."

"Yes, perhaps they should have waited for us to make sense of what was going on," said a B, in support.

"We should have stopped playing games with each other."

"Maybe it was a bit unfair overloading the Bs with questions and ridiculous messages," offered another.

"Nothing!" came another suggestion.

"What, you couldn't have done anything different?" challenged another C.

"I don't think so," said the C.

The challenger responded. "But you were as involved as the rest of us in playing up. You could have stopped."

"Given everything we have talked about today, I don't believe we would have behaved any differently. We wanted to do something, in fact, I needed to do something, so I did – we all did," she replied.

"Therefore," I said, trying to wrap this up, "we all potentially became busy fools because we needed to remind people, our boss included, that our time was valuable. We needed to let them know that there were only so many hours in the day, and so many things we could work on within those hours. Of course, this has another benefit to us; it allows us some breathing space for thinking time. In essence, we buy ourselves some freedom by looking busy."

"Thinking time?" questioned a C. "We don't have time to think."

The room paused.

"Have you ever heard the expression: Don't just sit there – do something?" I asked. "People used to say it to me all the time when I was growing up. I have a different view. Maybe it should be: Don't just do something – sit there! Take time out to think about what you have been doing and how you have been doing it. Then think about what you want to do and how you want to do it. Today is very much about that: taking time out to explore what we are doing and how we are doing it."

This caught their attention.

"However, on reflection, I can't see the Cs could have done anything differently for all the reasons previously discussed," I added. "Let's leave it there for now."

The group agreed to move on.

CAPTURING THE MOMENT

"Over the previous few hours we've experienced how different levels in an organisation behave. We've had a discussion about how we all felt, and started to understand what may have caused us to feel that way. I'm keen to capture all of this before we lose it, so let's now think about all the messages that came out of playing the game. What are the key messages for you?" I asked.

And so I returned to a blank flip chart and, for the next 15 minutes, I wrote furiously.

"Make sure you communicate," came the first suggestion.

"And make it clear," added the next.

"When you communicate, it should be consistent." "Yes, give everyone the same message."

"Following on from that, don't assume everyone will have the same interpretation of the message."

"Then check for their understanding."

"If that's the case, then we have to wait for a clear direction," offered another C.

"It's uncomfortable not knowing what's going on." "Challenge our paradigms; A could have walked the floor."

"Perhaps challenge each other; don't just accept what someone says as reality."

"Ask why."

"We need to involve people."

"Therefore delegate and empower people." "Collaborate across the teams."

"Develop a system that everyone understands."

"If we have the right system, then assign roles and responsibilities within the system."

"Be prepared to take risks."

"The right risks though," added A.

"People don't thrive on uncertainty; they do thrive on assurances and certainty, though!"

"Make effective use of what you have; don't waste it." "How about everyone should be their own leader?" "In the unknown, people behave differently."

"Once the direction is set, it can be difficult to turn it around."

"People need recognition."

"We all need meaningfulness."

"Managers need to let go!"

After an initial flurry of suggestions, at this point the group started to slow down, so I decided to help for a moment.

"What did you find easy to do, then?" I asked. "It was easy to play a game!"

"Yes, looking busy doing nothing!"

"I found it easy not to participate if I wanted to."

"It seemed easy to create chaos very quickly."

"At times it was easy to panic under pressure."

"During the review session it was easy to get into a blame culture."

"It was easy to get sidetracked, and to sidetrack others."

"It was easy to mistrust others."

"And, of course, now it's easy to see where we were going wrong!"

"Okay, okay!" I said, holding my hands up in mock surrender. "On that note I think we can stop there. I'm sure we could come up with many more learning points from the game if we carried on, but I believe we have enough here to work with," and I pointed to the flip charts on which I had captured all the learning points.

Key Learning Points

- Clear communication
- Consistency of communication
- Don't assume anything
- Check that everyone has the same understanding
- Wait for a clear direction
- It's uncomfortable not knowing what's going on
- Challenge each other
- Ask: Why?
- Involve others
- Delegate to others
- Empower others
- Collaborate across teams
- Develop an understandable system
- Assign roles and responsibilities
- Be prepared to take risks
- The right risks
- People don't thrive on uncertainty
- Make effective use of what you have
- Everyone should be their own leader
- In the unknown people behave differently
- Once direction is set, it can be difficult to turn it around
- Cs need recognition
- Need meaningfulness across all roles
- Managers need to let go
- Humans have a tendency to overcomplicate things

What We Found Easy

- Easy to play a game!
- It was easy looking busy doing nothing
- Easy not to participate
- Easy to create chaos
- At times easy to panic
- Easy to get into blame culture
- Easy to get sidetracked
- Easy to sidetrack others
- Easy to mistrust others
- Easy to see where we were going wrong

CLOSING SPEECH

We spent the rest of the day discussing each of these key learning points and formulated individual, team and organisational actions to address some of the main issues that the group could identify were impacting on success.

Towards the end of the day I pulled Brian to one side. "Brian, we are nearing the end of the day now and I would like you to close the event. Can you think about how you want to sum up what you and your team have experienced, and maybe highlight some of the most important messages you have taken from the day? Is that okay with you?" I asked.

"Absolutely fine," he said, "I know what I want to say already."

"Great, I'll wrap things up and hand over to you, then."

"Before we hear the final words from Brian," I started, "I want to take us back to the reason we came together here today. Brian and his exec team recognised that there was a problem with the way the business was performing, but couldn't put their finger on what the cause of the problem was. Today was about helping to work through step 2 of the six plus three step process to resolving an organisational problem. I believe today will have helped to achieve step 2. I also believe you have moved into step 4."

I carried on: "I'm pleased with how you have progressed and the work you have all put into the day, but regrettably it's not enough." I paused before going on. "Having an enjoyable day is only the start of things. It's what you do with what you have learned today that's important. I will remind you of just one of your key learning points from playing the game: everyone should be their own leader. Therefore, it's up to all of you to do what you say you are going to do and make this company a great company, as it rightly deserves to be. That's all from me. I will see you all in the future as we go through your transformation together." I sat down and let Brian speak to his team.

"I have been asked to summarise the event and the key messages I have taken from the day. I can sum it up with just one single but vital factor that I now recognise has a major impact on the success of an organisation." He hesitated and looked at each and every person in the room before saying: "I realise that as I've climbed through the levels in organisations and am now where I am, I had forgotten what it was like to be one of the workforce. I had forgotten what the workforce needed to enable them to fully engage and flourish. Their need is great. As a C in the game, I behaved like any C would have behaved under those circumstances. I now realise that I, we, as a leadership team, are not just part of the problem – our behaviour IS the problem. My overriding message from today, one that every one of us must remember, is very simple but immensely powerful and all-encompassing."

"So what is it?" I asked. "What is your key message? Please share it with everyone."

"Simple," he said, "never forget what it's like to be a C. That's it, plain and simple."

To learn more about how the 'Game' can transform your organisation, and experience first hand this phenomenal eye-opener to organisational behaviour, please visit:
trevorjarrett.co.uk or
changecreation.co.uk
or call Trevor Jarrett's office: 0044 (0)1277 656662